REPARENTING YOUR WOUNDED INNER CHILD

EXPLORE CHILDHOOD AND GENERATIONAL TRAUMA
TO BREAK DESTRUCTIVE PATTERNS, BUILD
EMOTIONAL STRENGTH, AND ACHIEVE PERSONAL
GROWTH WITH 7 EMPOWERING STEPS

LEIGH W. HART

401
—Publishing—

CONTENTS

Introduction   13

Part I
BUILDING A FOUNDATION

1. THE CHILD IN THE MIRROR   21
Emily's Story   22
What Is the Inner Child?   23
What Is Inner Child Work?   24
Myths and Frequently Asked Questions   29
Interactive Element   31

2. THE INNER CHILD IN THE DRIVER'S SEAT   35
Christine's Story   36
Unearthing the Past: Understanding Childhood Trauma   37
The Holmes and Rahe Stress Scale   38
Stress in Childhood   40
The Impact of a Negative or Traumatic Experience   42
Negative Patterns   44
Attachment Styles and Childhood Trauma   46
Characteristics of a Healthy Inner Child   49
Why Is My Inner Child Unhealthy?   51
Why You Need a Healthy Inner Child Ruling Your Life   52
Interactive Element   54

3. THE ART OF REPARENTING   57
Reparenting With Compassion   59
The Power of Self-Love   61
Creating a Self-Nurturing Routine   63
Embrace the Healing Journey   65
The Inner Child Healing Timeline   67
Interactive Element   68

4. RESISTANCE AND SELF-SABOTAGE   73
   Making the Unconscious Conscious   74
   Types of Challenges to Be Prepared For   76
   Recognizing Self-Sabotage and What to Do
   About It   78
   Interactive Element   81

Part II
LET THE HEALING BEGIN

5. STEP ONE—RECONNECT WITH YOUR INNER
   CHILD   87
   Michelle's Story   88
   Benefits of Reconnecting With Your Inner Child   91
   Signs You Are Disconnected From Your Inner
   Child   92
   How to Reconnect With Your Inner Child   94
   Interactive Element   96

6. STEP TWO—HOW TO UNEARTH AND
   UNDERSTAND YOUR INNER CHILD'S
   HIDDEN WOUNDS   103
   Unveiling the Unseen Scars of Your Inner Child   105
   Exploring the Origins of Hidden Wounds   110
   Uncovering Hidden Wounds Through Inner
   Child Work   112
   Exercises to Help Process Trauma   114
   Therapeutic Techniques and Professional
   Support   116
   Thomas' Story   120
   Interactive Element   122

7. STEP THREE—BEING THE PARENT YOU
   NEEDED BACK THEN   127
   Juan's Journey to Healing   128
   Sophia's Path to Renewal   129
   Good Parents Versus Bad Parents   130
   The Power of Reparenting for Self-Healing   131
   Reconstructing and Reparenting   132
   Interactive Element   134

8. STEP FOUR—HEALING EMOTIONAL
   TRIGGERS   141
   What Are Emotions?   142
   How to Cultivate Emotional Awareness and
   Mindfulness   144
   What Can We Do About Unwanted or Unhelpful
   Emotions?   145
   Emotional Release: Building a Safe Space to
   Prevent Further Repression   147
   How to Validate and Nurture Your Inner Child's
   Emotions   151
   Interactive Element   153

9. STEP FIVE—TRANSFORM NEGATIVE SELF-
   TALK   157
   What Is Negative Self-Talk   158
   Unhelpful Core Beliefs   159
   Our Inner Child's Hidden Beliefs and Behaviors
   and How to Change Them   160
   Interactive Element   163

10. STEP SIX—THE BOUNDARY LINE   167
    The Significance of Defining Boundaries   168
    The Difference Between Healthy and Unhealthy
    Boundaries   170
    How Does Our Childhood Impact Boundary
    Development?   171
    Recognizing Signs of Boundary Erosion or
    Violation and Maintaining Them   173
    Designing a Personalized Protection Plan For
    Your Inner Child   175
    Interactive Element   176

11. STEP SEVEN—LETTING GO OF THE PAST   179
    What Is Forgiveness and How Do We Forgive?   181
    How to Let Go of Shame and Guilt   184
    Interactive Element   186

Part III

FACING FORWARD

12. GROWING FROM STRENGTH TO STRENGTH 191
    How Embracing and Nurturing Our Inner Child
    Helps   192
    Embrace Vulnerability   193
    Embrace Resiliency   194
    Interactive Element   196

13. CELEBRATING AND POWERFULLY CREATING 199
    Why Do We Need to Celebrate?   200
    Embracing Transformative Growth and
    Wholeness   201
    Keep the Inner Child Healing Going   202
    Interactive Element   204

    Conclusion   207
    References   211

Elevate Your Journey With...

EXCLUSIVE COMPLIMENTARY
SUPPORT MATERIALS!

As a BONUS:

I have created a customized collection of
75+ journal pages and interactive worksheets that have been
designed to complement the steps, journal prompts, and exercises
discussed in this book perfectly.

Go to:
InnerChild.LeighWHart.com
to receive your FREE
printable support materials.

TRIGGER WARNING:

This book contains discussions regarding childhood traumas, abuse, toxic relationships, and other potentially emotionally triggering material. Please proceed with caution and stop reading if you feel overwhelmed. If you're in need of someone to speak to, you can reach the National Domestic Violence Hotline at 800-799-7233, or you can contact the Suicide and Crisis Lifeline at 988.

MEDICAL DISCLAIMER:

The content provided in this book is intended for educational and informational purposes. It is not a substitute for professional mental health advice, diagnosis, or treatment. Always consult with a qualified mental health professional or healthcare provider for personalized guidance regarding your specific mental health concerns. The author and publisher of this book do not endorse or recommend any specific therapies, medications, or interventions, and any decisions made based on the information presented in this book are at the reader's discretion and sole responsibility.

INTRODUCTION

Caring for your inner child has a powerful and surprisingly quick result: Do it, and the child heals.

— MARTHA BECK

Within each of us lies a fragment of our past, an echo of our childhood experiences that lingers in the corners of our hearts. This aspect of ourselves is our inner child, a wellspring of creativity, joy, and boundless enthusiasm. Yet, like delicate porcelain, this inner child can bear the marks of old wounds, fears, and traumas. If we dare to listen, we can hear its whispers in our thoughts and feel its presence in our actions. This book, *Reparenting Your Wounded Inner Child*, invites you to embark on a transformative journey to heal, nurture, and empower that inner child within you.

We all have a part of ourselves that connects back to our childhood. This inner child is the canvas upon which our adult lives are painted. Its experiences have positively and negatively shaped us, influencing our choices, relationships, and emotional well-being. The adventures and misadventures of our early years have woven a tapestry of memories, some vibrant with joy, while others are tinged with pain and fear.

But here's the truth: you hold the power to rewrite your story. It's not about erasing the past but about embracing the process of healing and transformation. If your inner child experienced trauma or fear, you may have developed coping mechanisms that once served as shields but now hold you back. Perhaps you've felt stuck, trapped in patterns of limiting beliefs and fears that seem insurmountable. The good news is that these patterns can be unraveled, and your inner child can be lovingly reparented to thrive once more.

The journey toward healing and self-discovery is sacred - paved with intention and compassion. As you turn the pages of this book, you'll find a comprehensive guide, a roadmap that leads you through seven empowering steps that will help you:

- Acknowledge past trauma's impact on behavior.
- Nurture your inner child through self-compassion.
- Dismantle harmful patterns and cultivate emotional resilience.
- Enhance relationships.
- Empower personal growth.
- Sustain progress through integration.

- Cultivate emotional well-being and personal development.

Each step tells a story of the strength within you. It's an opportunity to nurture the bond between your adult self and your inner child—a relationship built on trust, understanding, and unwavering support.

As you hold this book in your hands, a specific catalyst likely prompted you to seek its wisdom. It's not the title that resonated with you, but the yearning to mend the fragments within you, heal old wounds, and discover a new path to emotional well-being. You may have battled with fears, grappled with insecurities, or yearned for deeper connections. Whatever your catalyst, know that you are not alone. This is a safe space.

By embarking on this journey of reparenting your wounded inner child, you'll uncover shortcuts to profound transformation:

- Healing emotional wounds and trauma, embracing inner peace.
- Nurturing a healthy and loving relationship with yourself.
- Breaking free from negative patterns rooted in childhood experiences.
- Establishing and maintaining healthy boundaries in relationships.
- Cultivating self-compassion, self-love, and a positive self-image.

Throughout these pages, you'll encounter exercises, techniques, and journal prompts designed to guide you through actionable steps. Journaling is a gateway to deeper self-awareness, allowing you to process the revelations and results that will undoubtedly arise from your efforts.

To aid you further, I've prepared customized worksheets and journal pages available at InnerChild.LeighWHart.com. These tools are crafted to enhance your journey, empowering you to engage fully with the steps, exercises, and journal prompts within the book.

If you've read my first book, *Don't Get Derailed by Your Attachment Style*, you'll find that the concept of inner child healing is threaded through its pages. Insecurity in attachment often stems from childhood experiences, making inner child work a vital component of your healing journey.

Now, as you stand on the precipice of transformation, know you are supported in this endeavor. As you turn the page, you're stepping into a voyage of self-discovery, healing, and empowerment. In Part One of this book, you'll explore the essential foundation required for inner child healing, preparing you for the work to come. When you transition to Part Two, you will find the seven empowering steps that will lead you down your path of personal growth.

Your emotional strength, resilience, and self-awareness await you on the other side of healing. Embrace the journey and let the nurturing of your wounded inner child lead you to a life imbued with joy, authenticity, and profound transformation.

With heartfelt anticipation...

PART I

BUILDING A FOUNDATION

1

THE CHILD IN THE MIRROR

In every adult, there lurks a child—an eternal child, something that is always becoming, is never completed, and calls for unceasing care, attention, and education. That is the part of the personality which wants to develop and become whole.

— CARL JUNG

What is my inner child? How can I comprehend this aspect of myself? When I gaze into the mirror, I don't just see my physical reflection; I also encounter various facets of who I am, including an inner child who craves acknowledgment and assistance. I possess an inner child—an inherent component of my being. I must acknowledge and collaborate with this inner child to foster my personal growth.

EMILY'S STORY

In a small town surrounded by rolling hills lived Emily, a young girl with an extraordinary childhood marred by a toxic home. With an alcoholic father and an emotionally abusive mother, Emily learned early on that she must become the caregiver and protector for her younger siblings. At the tender age of seven, she shouldered adult responsibilities.

Her childhood was devoid of innocence; while other children played, Emily navigated chaos. She matured prematurely, neglecting the wonder, curiosity, and carefree joy of her inner child.

As she grew, the scars of her traumatic upbringing became evident. Trusting others was a challenge, and self-esteem was elusive. Her past haunted her relationships and prevented her from enjoying life's simple pleasures.

Determined not to be defined by her past, Emily embarked on a healing journey. Therapy helped her confront repressed memories and set boundaries. Mindfulness and self-compassion rebuilt her self-esteem. Pursuing neglected hobbies rekindled her creative spirit.

Over time, Emily's life transformed. Meaningful friendships, a loving partnership, and a thriving career emerged. Reconnecting with her inner child allowed her to laugh freely, embrace vulnerabilities, and relish life's joys.

Emily's story reminds us that even in darkness, light can be found. Through self-discovery, therapy, and nurturing her inner child, she not only survived her traumatic past but thrived in a life filled with love, happiness, and purpose.

WHAT IS THE INNER CHILD?

The inner child is a concept in psychology and therapy that represents the emotional and psychological aspects of your personality that are influenced by your childhood experiences. It encompasses the feelings, memories, and vulnerabilities from your early years that continue to shape your behavior and emotional responses as an adult.

Comparison of Inner Child vs. Inner Adult:

- **Inner child:** The inner child embodies qualities associated with childhood, such as innocence, curiosity, spontaneity, and vulnerability. It's the part of you that carries the emotional imprints of past experiences, both positive and negative, and can influence your reactions and decisions in the present.
- **Inner adult:** The inner adult, on the other hand, represents the mature, rational, and responsible aspects of your personality that develop as you grow and gain life experience. It's the part of you that can make informed decisions, set boundaries, and navigate adult life effectively.

We have to ask ourselves if there is a positive side to the inner child. And the answer is yes; there can be a positive side. It can bring creativity, spontaneity, and a sense of wonder into your life. Embracing your inner child can help you connect with your imagination, playfulness, and the ability to experience joy in simple things. It can also foster empathy and compassion by reconnecting you with the vulnerability and innocence you once had.

The idea here is not that you should completely discard or suppress your inner child but rather that healing and integrating your inner child is important for personal growth and emotional well-being. When your inner child carries unresolved traumas or negative patterns from the past, it can hinder your ability to function as a healthy, happy adult. Healing the inner child involves addressing these past wounds, acknowledging and processing emotions, and developing more beneficial coping mechanisms. It's about achieving a balance where your inner child's positive qualities can coexist with the wisdom and responsibility of your inner adult, allowing you to lead a fulfilling life.

WHAT IS INNER CHILD WORK?

Imagine yourself as a six-year-old, innocently playing with other kids in your kindergarten class on a sunny day. As you joyfully run around the playground, you suddenly trip and tumble to the ground. Laughter erupts from the other children, and you can feel your cheeks flush with embarrassment.

The specifics of that moment may have faded from your memory over time. You might not recall the exact faces of your classmates or even your precise age at the time. What lingers in your consciousness, however, are the vivid sensations of shame washing over you, the sting of tears welling up in your eyes, and the ache of a skinned knee. Perhaps you can even recollect silently promising yourself, "I'll never allow myself to look foolish like that again."

Though your knee eventually healed, the emotional scars endured and followed you into adulthood. They continue to affect your life, even when you are not consciously aware of it. Whether it's been two decades or five since that playground incident, your inner six-year-old still significantly influences your decisions and behaviors. It's as if that wounded child is in charge, making it challenging to seize opportunities and take risks despite not even remembering the original event on the playground that triggered this internal conflict.

Inner child work is a profound and introspective approach to understanding and healing our emotional wounds that originated in our childhood. Our inner child embodies the emotions, beliefs, and experiences we had during our formative years.

The essence of inner child work lies in acknowledging that many of our adult behaviors, reactions, and patterns are rooted in these early experiences. By exploring and reconnecting with our inner child, we can gain valuable insights into why we respond to certain situations the way we do. It's like journeying in time to revisit our past selves, understand our unmet needs, and provide the care and nurturing that might have been lacking during our upbringing.

Here's a closer look at what inner child work entails:

- **Recognition:** The first step is acknowledging the existence of your inner child. This involves accepting that your current emotional reactions, triggers, and behaviors are often rooted in childhood experiences.
- **Reconnection:** Inner child work involves reconnecting with your younger self, often through visualization or meditation. You seek to understand the emotions and needs that your inner child carried during those early years.
- **Reparenting:** Once you've connected with your inner child, the next step is to reparent yourself. This means providing the love, care, and support your childhood may have lacked. It's about healing those wounds and meeting your inner child's unmet needs.
- **Integration:** As you progress in inner child work, you aim to integrate the wisdom and healing from this process into your present life. This integration helps you make healthier choices, respond to triggers more consciously, and break free from old, limiting patterns.
- **Emotional release:** Throughout this journey, it's common to experience emotional releases—moments when long-buried feelings surface. These releases can be cathartic and healing.

By engaging in inner child work, you gain a deeper understanding of your psyche and begin dismantling the barriers that may have held you back.

Carl Jung's Historical and Scientific Influence

To understand the profound impact that Carl Jung has had on inner child work, we must first explore the historical and scientific context of both Jungian psychology and the concept of the inner child.

Carl Gustav Jung (1875-1961) was a Swiss psychiatrist and psychoanalyst who founded analytical psychology. He was a contemporary of Sigmund Freud, but his theories and approach to psychology differed significantly. Jung's work was instrumental in developing depth psychology, which explores the unconscious mind and the deeper layers of the human psyche (Pikorn, 2020).

Jung introduced several key concepts that are highly relevant to inner child work (Pikorn, 2020):

- **Collective unconscious:** Jung proposed a collective unconscious shared by all humans, containing universal symbols and archetypes. These archetypes, such as the mother, the father, the hero, and the child, represent fundamental human experiences and are deeply embedded in our psyches.
- **Individuation:** Jung believed that the path to psychological wholeness involved the process of individuation, which is the integration of the various aspects of one's personality, including the unconscious elements. This process helps individuals become their true, authentic selves.

- **Shadow work:** Jungian psychology emphasizes the importance of confronting and integrating one's shadow, the dark and hidden aspects of the personality. This process is essential for inner growth and self-awareness.

The concept of the inner child, which plays a central role in inner child work, was not directly developed by Carl Jung himself. Instead, it emerged as a psychological concept in the latter half of the 20th century. However, Jung's ideas laid the groundwork for the exploration of the inner child (Pikorn, 2020):

- **Archetypes and the child:** Jung's identification of the child archetype as one of the fundamental archetypes in the collective unconscious contributed to the understanding of the inner child. The child archetype represents innocence, spontaneity, and a sense of wonder.
- **Integration of the shadow:** Jung's emphasis on shadow work, the process of acknowledging and reconciling one's darker aspects, is closely related to inner child work. Often, the wounded inner child is a part of the shadow that requires attention and healing.
- **Psychological development:** Jung's stages of psychological development, such as the process of individuation, provided a framework for understanding how the inner child evolves over the course of a person's life. Inner child work often involves revisiting and healing past developmental stages.

MYTHS AND FREQUENTLY ASKED QUESTIONS

Let's review this therapeutic approach and some frequently asked questions and myths surrounding inner child work:

- **Why is inner child work important?:** Inner child work can help individuals address unresolved childhood trauma, improve self-esteem, build healthier relationships, and break free from negative patterns of behavior.
- **How do I know if I need inner child work?:** If you struggle with persistent emotional issues, self-sabotaging behavior, or difficulty in forming healthy relationships, inner child work may be beneficial. It's particularly helpful for those with a history of childhood trauma or neglect.
- **Is inner child work the same as regression therapy?:** Inner child work may involve regression techniques, but it is different from full-blown regression therapy. Inner child work focuses on healing and nurturing your inner child, while regression therapy often involves revisiting memories and experiences.
- **Can I do inner child work on my own?:** While some people can explore inner child work independently using self-help resources, working with a qualified therapist or counselor is often recommended, especially if you have complex emotional issues or trauma.
- **How long does inner child work take to see results?:** The timeline for inner child work varies from person to person. Some may experience positive changes

relatively quickly, while others may require months or even years of ongoing work to see significant results.

Myths and Misconceptions

Myth: Inner child work is just for people with severe childhood trauma.

- Inner child work can benefit anyone, not just those with extreme trauma. It can help people heal and grow from various childhood experiences, including neglect, emotional abuse, and even more common challenges.

Myth: Inner child work is all about revisiting painful memories.

- While some inner child work may involve exploring past traumas, the focus is on healing and nurturing rather than dwelling on pain. It's about understanding and releasing negative emotions to promote healing.

Myth: Inner child work is only for individuals with deep psychological issues.

- Inner child work can benefit people dealing with various issues, including self-esteem, relationships, and personal growth, not just those with severe psychological problems.

Myth: Inner child work is a quick fix for all problems.

- Inner child work is a process that requires time and commitment. It's not a magic solution to all life's problems, but it can be a valuable tool for personal development and healing.

Myth: You must regress to your childhood to do inner child work.

- While some techniques may involve regression, inner child work doesn't always require revisiting specific memories. It can also focus on understanding and nurturing your inner child's emotional needs in the present.

INTERACTIVE ELEMENT

Journaling Journey

Journaling is a vital tool in the process of inner child work, as it serves as a bridge between your conscious mind and the deeply buried emotions and memories of your past. Through the act of writing, you can gently coax your inner child to express their thoughts, fears, and unmet needs, creating a safe and non-judgmental space for self-discovery and healing. Journaling helps you identify patterns, triggers, and unresolved wounds from childhood, allowing you to cultivate empathy and understanding toward your younger self. Let's begin our journaling journey now!

Below, you will find ten helpful journal prompts to get you started:

1. How would you describe your childhood experiences?
2. What were your primary childhood needs?
3. In what ways did childhood play influence your current adult self?
4. If you were talking to your inner self today, what do you wish you could say?
5. Describe a typical day in the life of your inner child.
6. Share a time when you felt that your inner child was overlooked or disregarded.
7. Were there phases in your childhood when things had both bright and challenging moments?
8. Are there unresolved issues or past traumas that require your attention?
9. Enumerate five things that cause you distress.
10. What do you yearn to release or relinquish in your life?

Does My Inner Child Need Help?

Insert a Y (yes) or N (no) next to the questions geared toward your wounded inner child, such as:

- Do you struggle with low self-esteem?
- Do you often worry that the people in your life will eventually leave you?

- Do you allow yourself to feel guilty when you stand up for yourself?
- Do you constantly criticize yourself for being inadequate or unworthy?
- Do you find it difficult to trust yourself and other people?
- Are you an addict, or have you been addicted to something?
- Do you prioritize other people's needs over your own?
- Do you often struggle with feelings of insecurity?
- Have you experienced trauma or neglect during your childhood?
- Do you find it challenging to set healthy boundaries in your relationships?
- Are you prone to self-criticism and harsh self-judgment?

As we conclude this chapter, we've explored the understanding of the young, vulnerable part of ourselves that has often been overlooked or neglected. In the upcoming chapter, we'll explore how to take control of this inner child, for it is through this empowerment that we can heal, grow, and create a more fulfilling and harmonious adult life.

2

THE INNER CHILD IN THE DRIVER'S SEAT

So much of the healing of our world begins in healing the inner child who rarely, if ever, got to come out and play.

— VINCE GOWMON

I experience feelings of guilt and shame, along with a sense of disconnection. I struggle with managing my emotions, often dealing with heightened anxiety and depression, as well as occasional bouts of anger. I realize that even just one of these challenges can significantly impact my life, potentially making the difference between success and happiness or failure and misery—an unhealed inner child.

CHRISTINE'S STORY

Growing up in my childhood home was extremely challenging. My stepfather struggled with alcoholism, while my mother had a tendency to abuse prescription pills. From the tender age of seven, it seemed like I was the only one capable of maintaining any sense of responsibility within our household. I found myself not only taking care of my needs but also being responsible for both of them.

When I turned 17, I left home for the first time, driven by the affection of a boy who showed me love. Unfortunately, I repeated the same patterns by getting involved with a young man who coped with his emotions through excessive drinking. The first time I heard the ice clinking in his glass, I was filled with dread and anxiety, but I was too ashamed and embarrassed to confide in anyone. I couldn't help but blame myself, believing everyone would see me as foolish.

Whenever he drank himself into a stupor, I felt an overwhelming surge of anger inside me, making me feel utterly helpless and isolated once more. I sank into a deep abyss of depression for an extended period. It would take many years of therapy for me to recognize my self-worth and realize that I deserved a life filled with hope, love, and compassion.

UNEARTHING THE PAST: UNDERSTANDING
CHILDHOOD TRAUMA

Let's unearth the past and try to understand childhood trauma
better. It's essential to approach this topic with sensitivity
because childhood trauma can have profound and long-lasting
effects on a person's life.

Traumatic events are experiences that overwhelm a person's
ability to cope and can leave lasting emotional scars. Childhood
trauma refers to adverse experiences that occur during a
person's early years, typically before the age of 18. Trauma can
manifest in various forms, and what counts as traumatic can
vary from person to person. However, there are some common
traumatic events that experts have identified:

- **Physical abuse:** This involves any deliberate use of
  force causing injury or bodily harm to a child. It can
  include hitting, kicking, or any form of violence.
- **Sexual abuse:** Sexual abuse encompasses any non-
  consensual sexual activity involving a child. It can range
  from molestation to rape.
- **Emotional abuse:** Be mindful that emotional abuse can
  be just as harmful as physical or sexual abuse. It
  includes constant criticism, humiliation, rejection, or
  any behavior undermining a child's self-worth.
- **Neglect:** Neglect is the failure of caregivers to provide
  for a child's basic needs, such as food, shelter, love, and
  emotional support.

- **Witnessing violence:** Children who witness domestic violence or community violence can experience trauma, even if they are not directly harmed.
- **Loss or abandonment:** The loss of a parent, caregiver, or close family member through death, divorce, or abandonment can be traumatic for a child.
- **Natural disasters or accidents:** Experiencing a natural disaster or a severe accident can also be traumatic for children.

Understanding the impact of trauma on children requires considering their developmental stages and age-appropriate responses.

THE HOLMES AND RAHE STRESS SCALE

The Holmes and Rahe Stress Scale, also known as the Social Readjustment Rating Scale (SRRS), was originally developed in 1967 by psychiatrists Thomas Holmes and Richard Rahe to assess the stress levels of adults. It is a tool that assigns numerical values to various life events based on the perceived stress associated with them, and individuals can use it to calculate their cumulative stress scores. The scale was primarily designed for use with adults to assess the potential risk of stress-related illnesses (Mind Tools Content Team, n.d.-b). I would like to advise all readers that I will include a copy of the SRRS test along with your free materials at InnerChild.LeighWHart.com.

While the Holmes and Rahe Stress Scale was not specifically developed for children, some modified versions have been created to assess stress in children and adolescents. These modified scales consider age-appropriate life events and stressors children may experience, such as academic pressures, family changes, peer relationships, and more.

We can adapt the scale to understand the impact of events at different stages of childhood:

Infancy (0-2 years):

- **Positive events:** Loving and consistent caregiving, nurturing, bonding.
- **Negative events:** Neglect, abuse, separation from primary caregivers.

Early Childhood (3-6 years):

- **Positive events:** Positive reinforcement, social interaction, learning through play.
- **Negative events:** Physical or emotional abuse, parental divorce, major illnesses.

Middle Childhood (7-11 years):

- **Positive events:** Academic achievements, forming friendships, feeling supported.
- **Negative events:** Bullying, parental conflicts, exposure to community violence.

Adolescence (12-18 years):

- **Positive events:** Academic success, autonomy, healthy relationships, support for identity development.
- **Negative events:** Peer pressure, substance abuse, academic failures, sexual assault.

Remember that children are resilient, but the impact of trauma can vary widely. Supportive, caring adults, therapy, and early intervention can make a significant difference in a child's ability to heal and thrive after experiencing trauma.

STRESS IN CHILDHOOD

It's important to recognize that some form of stress or negative experience in childhood is indeed inevitable. The journey from childhood to adulthood is fraught with challenges, and each child's experience is unique.

Even the happiest of childhoods can, at times, cause some form of trauma. This may sound counterintuitive, but it's essential to understand that it's not necessarily the event that determines the impact level. It's the individual's subjective experience of the event that plays a pivotal role. What might seem insignificant to one person could deeply affect another. This is why it's crucial not to judge or downplay someone's experiences.

Some children are naturally more resilient than others and can weather similar events with less negative impact. Resilience is a complex trait influenced by genetics, environment, and individual coping mechanisms. However, even the most resilient individuals can be affected by certain circumstances.

Let's explore some universal emotional wounds that can cause a form of trauma:

- **Betrayal:** Experiencing betrayal as a child, whether by a caregiver, friend, or family member, can create deep emotional scars. Trust is a fundamental part of human relationships, and when it's broken, it can lead to lasting emotional trauma.
- **Injustice:** Witnessing or experiencing injustice, such as unfair treatment or discrimination, can profoundly impact a child's sense of fairness and justice. It can lead to anger, powerlessness, and a skewed worldview.
- **Humiliation:** Humiliation can be incredibly damaging, especially in a social context. Being publicly shamed or ridiculed can lead to shame and low self-esteem that persist into adulthood.
- **Abandonment:** Feeling abandoned by caregivers can lead to attachment issues and emotional scars that affect relationships throughout life. The fear of abandonment can become a driving force in one's behavior and relationships.
- **Rejection:** Whether it's rejection by peers, romantic partners, or even family members, the experience of being rejected can be emotionally devastating. It can create feelings of unworthiness and isolation.
- **Neglect:** Physical or emotional neglect can have long-lasting consequences. Children consistently ignored or

left to fend for themselves may struggle with self-care, self-worth, and forming healthy relationships.

Understanding that these experiences can cause trauma, regardless of the outward appearance of a happy childhood, is vital for providing support and empathy to individuals who have endured such challenges.

THE IMPACT OF A NEGATIVE OR TRAUMATIC EXPERIENCE

Let's explore how negative or traumatic experiences can create emotional blockages and adult patterns. First and foremost, I want to acknowledge that discussing these topics can be challenging, but it's an essential step toward understanding and healing.

Imagine emotions as a flowing river. When we're born, this river is pure and unrestricted, allowing our feelings to flow freely. However, life is filled with experiences, both positive and negative, which shape our emotional landscape.

Negative or traumatic experiences, particularly during childhood, can act as dams in this river, hindering the natural flow of emotions. Here's how this process unfolds:

- **The initial impact:** Traumatic experiences, such as abuse, loss, or neglect, can be overwhelming and frightening. These experiences often leave a deep emotional scar, making it difficult to process and express our feelings.

- **Defense mechanisms:** We develop defense mechanisms to protect ourselves from the pain associated with these traumatic memories. These mechanisms may include denial, repression, or dissociation, which effectively block out the emotions tied to the trauma.
- **Formation of emotional blockages:** Over time, these defense mechanisms become habitual, forming emotional blockages. These blockages act like dams in our emotional river, preventing us from fully experiencing and expressing our emotions.
- **Impact on adult patterns:** As we grow into adulthood, these emotional blockages can have a profound impact on our behavior and relationships. For example, someone who experienced abandonment as a child might develop trust issues, affecting their ability to form healthy relationships. Others may struggle with anxiety or depression because of repressed emotions.
- **Repetition of patterns:** Unresolved emotional issues often lead to the repetition of patterns. People may find themselves attracted to situations or relationships that recreate the trauma, unknowingly seeking an opportunity for resolution or validation.

So, what can be done to address these emotional blockages and adult patterns? Let's review some steps:

- **Self-awareness:** Recognizing that you have emotional blockages and adult patterns is the first step. Self-awareness allows you to understand the root causes of your behaviors and reactions.

- **Seek support:** Reach out to a therapist or counselor who specializes in trauma and emotional healing. They can provide guidance and tools to help you navigate these complex emotions.
- **Express emotions:** Learn healthy ways to express your emotions. This could include journaling, art, or even talking with a trusted friend or therapist. You can gradually release the emotional blockages by acknowledging and processing your feelings.
- **Mindfulness and meditation:** Practices like mindfulness and meditation can help you stay present and connect with your emotions in a non-judgmental way. They can also reduce the impact of past trauma on your present life.
- **Professional help:** In some cases, trauma therapy techniques such as EMDR (Eye Movement Desensitization and Reprocessing) or exposure therapy may be necessary to work through specific traumatic memories.

NEGATIVE PATTERNS

Let's embark on a journey together to explore common unhealthy patterns that many people carry within themselves and what this means for the healing needs of our inner child. With compassion and understanding, we'll delve into the intricacies of these patterns, particularly those rooted in fear reactions.

It's a pattern we often see in people's lives. The compulsion to control situations and people to feel safe. In everyday relationships, this can manifest as micromanaging at work or overbearing behavior with family and friends. Our inner child, scarred by past experiences, believes control is the only way to prevent harm. Healing our inner child means teaching them true safety comes from vulnerability and trust, not control.

Toxic Family Patterns

These patterns are like a generational curse passed down from one generation to the next. Families often perpetuate the same inner child wounds, creating a cycle that seems impossible to break. Inner-child healing involves recognizing these patterns and consciously choosing to break the chain. It means acknowledging the pain and trauma of our ancestors and deciding to heal for ourselves and future generations.

Helplessness and Victim Mode

When faced with challenges, some of us slip into a state of helplessness and victimhood. We might blame others, become defensive, or employ various self-protection mechanisms. These patterns can be traced back to our inner child's fear of being hurt or rejected. Inner-child healing requires us to comfort that wounded inner child, to assure them that they are not helpless victims, and to empower them to respond to life's challenges from a place of strength.

Patterns in Intimate Relationships

Romantic relationships can bring out the worst in our wounded inner child. This is because they often require us to be vulnerable and emotionally open, which can trigger our deepest fears of rejection and abandonment. We may find ourselves repeating familiar relationship patterns, seeking love and validation in all the wrong places. Inner-child healing in the context of romantic relationships involves recognizing these triggers, working through them, and learning to love ourselves so that we can love others more authentically.

Love Languages

Our love languages, the ways we express and receive love, are often influenced by our childhood experiences. If we didn't receive certain types of love as children, we may unconsciously try to give that love to others in our adult relationships. Understanding our love languages can be a powerful tool in inner child healing. It allows us to recognize what we're missing and seek out healthy ways to fulfill those needs within ourselves and through our relationships.

ATTACHMENT STYLES AND CHILDHOOD TRAUMA

In the intricate tapestry of human relationships, one thread that often goes unnoticed but plays a profound role is our attachment style. Our early experiences, especially those in childhood, can significantly influence how we form and maintain connections with others throughout our lives. This concept is at the heart of Attachment Theory, a psychological framework that sheds light on how past experiences shape adult relationships.

Attachment Theory, pioneered by John Bowlby and expanded upon by Mary Ainsworth, explores how infants and children bond with their caregivers. It details how these early bonds serve as templates for our future relationships. Of these templates, we all aspire to have secure attachments in our relationships. However, if we don't naturally embody a secure attachment style, we may find ourselves in one of the insecure attachment styles: Anxious, Avoidant, or Fearful/Disorganized (*Attachment Trauma*, 2022).

- **Anxious attachment:** Individuals with an anxious attachment style tend to be overly preoccupied with their relationships. They often fear abandonment, constantly seek reassurance, and may become clingy or dependent on their partners. This attachment style often stems from inconsistent caregiving in childhood.
- **Avoidant attachment:** Those with an avoidant attachment style tend to emphasize their independence and self-sufficiency. They may be uncomfortable with emotional intimacy, resist opening up to others, and may prioritize self-reliance over close relationships. This attachment style can develop from caregivers who were emotionally unavailable.
- **Fearful/disorganized attachment:** This attachment style is characterized by a conflicting mix of anxious and avoidant tendencies. People with a

fearful/disorganized attachment may struggle with unpredictable and confusing behavior in relationships. Childhood trauma or abuse often underlies this attachment style.

- **Secure attachment:** This attachment style is a healthy and adaptive emotional bond that forms between infants or young children and their primary caregivers. It serves as a foundation for healthy social and emotional development throughout a person's life. This is considered the ideal attachment style. Understanding and fostering secure attachment is vital for promoting healthy emotional development and relationships.

Now, you might be wondering how childhood trauma fits into this equation. Well, childhood trauma can be a significant factor in the development of insecure attachment styles. Traumatic experiences in childhood, such as neglect, abuse, or inconsistent caregiving, can disrupt the healthy formation of attachment bonds. As a result, adults who have experienced childhood trauma may find themselves struggling with these insecure attachment styles in their adult relationships.

If you're looking to explore this topic in greater detail, I invite you to explore my book, *Don't Get Derailed by Your Attachment Style*. Within its pages, you'll find an in-depth exploration of how childhood trauma can specifically affect your attachment style in all types of adult relationships. Moreover, the book offers valuable insights and effective steps you can take to address insecure attachment issues in adulthood.

Inner child healing involves reconnecting with and healing the wounded aspects of your inner child—the younger, vulnerable version of yourself who experienced the trauma. Through self-awareness, therapy, and self-compassion, individuals can work toward resolving past wounds and fostering more secure and confident relationships.

CHARACTERISTICS OF A HEALTHY INNER CHILD

Let's explore the characteristics of a healthy inner child, which are typically present when past trauma or unhelpful learned patterns have been managed and processed. Our inner child represents the purest and most authentic part of ourselves, often shaped by our early experiences and emotional development. When we successfully navigate and heal from past wounds or limiting beliefs, we can cultivate a healthy inner child, which can greatly contribute to our overall well-being and personal growth.

- **Trust and openness:** A healthy inner child is marked by a sense of trust in oneself and others. It's the ability to open up to new experiences, people, and relationships without excessive fear or skepticism. This trust allows for deeper connections and a more positive outlook on life.
- **Playfulness, creativity, and spontaneity:** Playfulness is a fundamental quality of a healthy inner child. It involves a sense of wonder, imagination, and the ability to engage in activities for pure joy rather than for any specific purpose. Creativity flows naturally from this

state, as does spontaneity, allowing for thought and action flexibility.

- **Emotional expression and authenticity:** A healthy inner child can express emotions freely and authentically. It's not burdened by the need to suppress feelings or hide vulnerabilities. This emotional openness leads to more meaningful connections with others and a deeper understanding of oneself.
- **Curiosity and exploration:** Curiosity is the driving force behind personal growth and learning. A healthy inner child is naturally curious and eager to explore new ideas, experiences, and the world around them. This curiosity fosters ongoing personal development and a zest for life.
- **Flexibility and adaptability:** A key characteristic of a healthy inner child is flexibility and adaptability. This means being able to navigate life's challenges with resilience and a positive attitude. It involves the ability to bounce back from setbacks, adjust to change, and embrace new opportunities.

In essence, a healthy inner child represents a state of emotional balance and psychological well-being. When past trauma or unhelpful learned patterns have been managed and processed, these qualities can flourish, allowing us to lead more fulfilling and joyful lives.

WHY IS MY INNER CHILD UNHEALTHY?

Let's look at a deeply personal and sensitive topic: the recognition of unhealthy aspects of your inner child that stem from the negative emotional and psychological impact of childhood trauma. This is not an easy subject to discuss, but understanding these aspects is crucial for healing and personal growth.

- **Core wounds and unresolved traumas:** Imagine your inner child as a repository of all your good and bad experiences. Childhood trauma can create deep emotional wounds that fester over time. These core wounds may manifest as feelings of unworthiness, abandonment, shame, or fear. They influence your choices, relationships, and self-perception, often without you even realizing it.
- **Emotional reactivity and triggers:** Your inner child carries the emotional baggage from past traumas. When confronted with situations that remind you of those painful moments, your emotional reactions can be intense and disproportionate. These triggers can lead to outbursts of anger, sadness, or anxiety, which may seem irrational to others but are very real for you.
- **Limiting beliefs and negative self-talk:** Childhood trauma often plants seeds of self-doubt and negative self-perception. You may internalize messages like "I'm not good enough" or "I'm unlovable." These limiting beliefs can hold you back from pursuing your dreams and hinder your self-esteem.

- **Defense mechanisms and coping strategies:** To protect oneself from further harm, your inner child develops defense mechanisms and coping strategies during traumatic experiences. These might include avoidance, denial, perfectionism, or people-pleasing. While these mechanisms may have been essential for survival during childhood, they can become counterproductive in adulthood, hindering personal growth and authentic relationships.
- **Patterns of self-sabotage and self-destructive behaviors:** Unresolved childhood trauma can lead to patterns of self-sabotage and self-destructive behaviors. These actions may be attempts to cope with emotional pain or recreate familiar dynamics from the past. For instance, you might find yourself repeating unhealthy relationship patterns or turning to substance abuse to numb your pain.

Recognizing these unhealthy aspects of your inner child can be a challenging process. It often involves introspection, therapy, and a willingness to confront painful memories.

WHY YOU NEED A HEALTHY INNER CHILD RULING YOUR LIFE

I would like to have a look at the unmanaged, unsupported, and unrecognized inner child and why you don't want this vulnerable part of yourself to be in control of your life. The inner child is a concept that many psychologists and therapists refer to, representing the childlike aspect of our psyche that carries our early experiences, emotions, and wounds. Here's why it's crucial to take charge and not let this inner child run the show.

When the inner child is left unmanaged and unchecked, it can keep you stuck at an immature emotional level. The appropriate emotional responses for a child may not serve you well as an adult. Unmanaged inner children often react to situations with the same intensity as when they were initially wounded, leading to overreactions and irrational behaviors.

Many adults are unconsciously controlled by their inner child. This means that the decisions you make are heavily influenced by the emotional wounds and traumas from your past. These inner children are not rational or logical; they are driven by the emotions experienced during pain and hurt.

When your inner child is in charge, it carries a backpack full of unresolved emotions—anger, shame, and sometimes even rage. These emotions can bubble up unexpectedly, causing outbursts, conflicts, and self-destructive behaviors. They can also cloud your judgment and affect your relationships, both personal and professional.

Your inner child serves as the lens through which you view and make decisions in your adult life. If your inner child is wounded, it might make choices based on fear, insecurity, or the need for validation rather than on what is genuinely best for you. This can lead to a cycle of making poor decisions that reinforce negative patterns.

Unmanaged inner children can wreak havoc on your relationships. They can cause you to repeat unhealthy relationship patterns or push away people who genuinely care about you. When your inner child is in control, it can be challenging to have healthy, mature relationships because your emotional reactions may be disproportionate to the situation.

So, it's clear that allowing your unmanaged, unsupported, and unrecognized inner child to control your life is not a recipe for happiness or success. Instead, it's essential to acknowledge and work with your inner child, providing the support and healing it needs. This involves seeking therapy, practicing self-awareness, and learning to make decisions from a place of emotional maturity rather than reacting from past wounds.

INTERACTIVE ELEMENT

Self-Assessment: Could My Inner Child be in Control?

I would like you to continue your journaling journey while you work through this self-assessment. Let's look at some prompts to get you started:

1. Do I often react to situations with strong emotions that feel disproportionate to the circumstances, such as anger, fear, or sadness?
2. Is it challenging for me to plan for the future or set long-term goals, as if I'm unsure of what I want as an adult?
3. Do I struggle with setting and maintaining healthy boundaries with people in my life?

4. Do I have difficulty making decisions and often feel overwhelmed by choices, no matter how small?
5. Do I avoid confronting or addressing conflicts in my relationships, hoping they will resolve themselves?
6. Do I find it challenging to handle stress and tend to cope through avoidance or distraction rather than constructive methods?
7. Am I drawn to activities or behaviors that provide immediate gratification but may not be in my long-term best interest?
8. Do I often feel a sense of nostalgia or longing for the past, perhaps yearning for the simplicity of childhood?
9. Do I tend to blame myself excessively when things go wrong, even when it's not entirely my fault?
10. Do I struggle to express my needs and desires assertively, sometimes resorting to passive-aggressive communication or withdrawal?

As I sat there, feeling the unmistakable presence of my inner child firmly in the driver's seat, I couldn't help but acknowledge the profound journey of self-discovery that lay ahead. The wheel was in their tiny hands, and I understood that it was time to embark on the art of reparenting. In the next chapter, we will explore the transformative power of nurturing and healing the wounded aspects of ourselves, learning to provide the love, care, and guidance we so desperately needed as children. Just as a skilled artist meticulously restores a masterpiece, we too can reclaim the beauty of our inner world through reparenting, unveiling the vibrant colors of resilience and self-love hidden beneath the layers of time.

3

THE ART OF REPARENTING

I learned that even though I have a very different personality from my parents, the way I treat my inner child is no different than how my parents treated me. I have unconsciously adopted some beliefs and habits from my parents. It's as though they continue to live within me.

— YONG KANG CHAN

By becoming aware of our inner child and giving it what it needs, we can, as mature adults, fulfill the role of the parent and parenting care and love that we needed but perhaps never got as children.

Imagine your inner child as a part of you that carries the emotional wounds and pain from your past. These wounds often stem from experiences that were hurtful, neglectful, or even traumatic. Reparenting is like giving your wounded inner child the love, care, and support you needed but might not have received when you were younger.

Now, I want to emphasize something crucial: When you're reparenting, it's essential to approach it with kindness and gentleness. You're right; you cannot use the same harshness or behaviors that might have caused the pain in the first place. Force and fear have no place in this healing process.

Think of it as if you're nurturing a fragile plant. You wouldn't yell at it to grow faster, right? Instead, you'd give it sunlight, water, and nourishment. The same principle applies here. Your inner child needs love, understanding, and patience to heal.

Let's review a few steps to keep in mind as you embark on your reparenting journey:

- **Self-compassion:** Start by being compassionate with yourself. Understand that the wounds you carry are not your fault. Treat yourself as you would a dear friend going through a tough time.
- **Inner dialogue:** Pay attention to your inner dialogue. Replace self-criticism and negative self-talk with kind and supportive words. Encourage yourself as you would encourage a child you care deeply about.
- **Emotional validation:** Allow yourself to feel your emotions without judgment. It's okay to be sad, angry, or scared sometimes. These feelings are valid and acknowledging them is a crucial part of healing.

- **Reparenting practices:** Engage in activities that bring you comfort and joy. This could be journaling, meditation, art, or spending time in nature. These practices are aimed to help you reconnect with your inner child.
- **Seeking help:** If needed, consider seeking the support of a therapist or counselor who specializes in inner child work. They can provide guidance and a safe space for your healing journey.

REPARENTING WITH COMPASSION

I want to talk to you about something fundamental: reparenting yourself with compassion. It's a journey of self-discovery and self-care that can truly transform your life. So, grab a cup of tea or your favorite beverage, and let's dive into the world of self-compassion and self-worth.

Let's take a moment to reflect on how you treat yourself when things don't go as planned. Do you tend to be overly critical, blaming yourself for every misstep or failure? Well, you're not alone in this. Many of us struggle with self-criticism, but the good news is that you can change that narrative.

Self-compassion is like a soothing balm for your soul. It's about treating yourself with the same kindness and understanding you'd offer to a dear friend going through a tough time. And guess what? Research shows that it's not just a feel-good concept—it has tangible benefits for your mental and emotional well-being (*4 Ways to Boost Your Self-Compassion*, 2021).

When you embrace self-compassion, you're likely to experience lower levels of anxiety and depression. Why? Because you acknowledge your suffering and respond to it with kindness. Instead of spiraling into self-criticism, you become your own source of comfort and support.

Now, let's get practical. How can you boost your self-compassion skills? Here are four simple yet effective ways to get started:

- **Comfort your body:** Your physical well-being is closely linked to your emotional state. When you're feeling down, take care of your body. Eat something nutritious, rest if you're tired, give yourself a relaxing self-massage, or take a leisurely walk. Remember, nurturing your body is an act of self-compassion.
- **Write a letter to yourself:** Think of a painful situation from your past—maybe a breakup, job loss, or a toxic childhood memory. Now, write a letter to yourself about it, but here's the key: don't assign blame, not to others and certainly not to yourself. Instead, focus on nurturing your feelings and offering yourself understanding and support.
- **Give yourself encouragement:** Imagine your best friend facing a challenging situation. What would you say to them? Now, when you find yourself in a similar situation, direct those same compassionate responses toward yourself. Be your own source of support, reminding yourself that you're doing the best you can.

- **Practice mindfulness:** Even just a few minutes of meditation or mindfulness exercises can work wonders. It's a way to connect with your inner self, acknowledge your pain or discomfort, and accept it without judgment. Mindfulness helps you stay present and compassionate toward yourself, even in difficult moments.

THE POWER OF SELF-LOVE

Let's dive into the wonderful world of self-love, a power that can truly transform your life. You know, sometimes we all think we understand self-love, but it's not always as clear as it seems. It's like knowing you should eat to nourish your body but not understanding the deep connection between self-love and everything else we strive for, like finding love, success, and happiness.

Ask yourself: how can we effectively love someone else before we've learned to love ourselves unconditionally? It's like trying to share a meal when your plate is empty. Our understanding of self-love often starts in childhood, picked up from those who cared for us. It's usually not something taught consciously; we simply observe how those around us express it.

Self-love goes way beyond fancy clothes and makeup. It's a term for all the ways we show love to ourselves, both physically and emotionally. You'd be surprised to find that many well-groomed individuals may not truly grasp what self-love entails. But here's the real gem: self-love isn't selfish. It's an act of kindness toward others because when you love yourself, you're less likely to burden others with your unresolved issues.

Self-love has four key aspects: self-worth, self-care, self-aware-ness, and self-esteem. All of these are like pieces of a puzzle, and when one is missing, the picture isn't complete. Achieving self-love is a journey that often mirrors confronting your inner demons. It's tough because it means letting go of things and people we're attached to. Our addiction to those things can lead us to love ourselves conditionally, trading true self-love for fleeting distractions.

Let's break down these aspects:

- **Self-worth:** Society often bombards us with negativity, making us focus on our flaws and projecting that onto ourselves. But here's the truth: You're born with endless potential. Self-worth is about believing in yourself, even when past experiences may make it challenging. Recognize the good things about you, and if you can't find them, ask others. You're worthy every single day.
- **Self-care:** This aspect leans more toward physical actions, but it's not solely about that. It includes things like taking care of your body, eating well, staying hydrated, and doing things you love. It also extends to what you consume mentally, like the music, media, and people you surround yourself with. Compared to the other aspects, self-care is often the easiest place to start your journey to self-love.
- **Self-awareness:** This is all about understanding your thought processes, emotions, and how they drive your

actions. Do you ever wonder why certain thoughts make you angry or happy? Self-awareness helps you navigate these emotions effectively. One way to boost self-awareness is by journaling your thoughts, emotions, and actions.

- **Self-esteem:** This stems from self-worth. When you truly value yourself, self-esteem naturally follows. It's tied to our achievements and qualities. Building self-esteem involves understanding that you're valuable, no matter your accomplishments or qualities. Remind yourself daily that you don't have to justify your existence through achievements.

Here's a transformative practice to steer you on your journey toward self-compassion: Pose this question to yourself, "What actions would someone who truly cares for themselves take?" This is akin to having your personal inner guide. Have faith in your intuition, even when it may lead you down unfamiliar paths. Always bear in mind that the voyage to self-love is a remarkable odyssey, and it commences with showering yourself with kindness. You've got the strength to embark on this journey!

CREATING A SELF-NURTURING ROUTINE

I'm glad you're taking the time to explore the idea of creating a self-nurturing routine. It's a wonderful step toward a happier and healthier you. I totally get it; life can be tough, and sometimes we forget to prioritize ourselves. But guess what? You are absolutely worthy of extra care and kindness, just like everyone else.

Let's talk about something essential first: the wounded inner child. Many of us carry some scars from our past, and those experiences can lead us to believe that we don't deserve self-care. Maybe you were told or made to feel like you weren't important or that your needs didn't matter. That can stick with you, but it's time to challenge those beliefs.

When your self-worth and confidence are low, one of the most powerful things you can do is to start treating yourself better. It's like building a strong foundation from the ground up. By taking small steps to nurture yourself, you're sending a powerful message to your inner self: "I am worthy of love and care."

Self-care isn't just a trendy buzzword; it's a vital part of emotional well-being. Let's reframe it to charge up those emotional batteries. When you neglect self-care, you can end up feeling drained, stressed, and overwhelmed. That's why we need to make it a part of your daily routine.

Now, let's dive a bit deeper into the mind-body link. Your emotional well-being is closely connected to your physical health. When you're stressed or anxious, your body can react with tension, headaches, or even digestive issues. On the flip side, when you engage in self-care activities like meditation, exercise, or spending time doing things you love, your body responds by releasing feel-good chemicals like endorphins, which reduce stress and boost your mood.

It's like a beautiful cycle: taking care of your emotional well-being through self-nurturing routines can lead to better physical health and vice versa. So, don't underestimate the power of a good night's sleep, a nourishing meal, or a relaxing bath. These simple acts of self-love can have a profound impact on how you feel, both mentally and physically.

We all have our struggles, and asking for support when needed is perfectly okay. Surround yourself with people who uplift and encourage you. I encourage you to start crafting a self-nurturing routine that works for you. You don't need to make this time-consuming or complicated. Start with small steps, like setting aside a few minutes each day to breathe deeply, journal your thoughts, or simply enjoy a cup of tea in peace. Gradually, you'll find that these self-care moments will boost your self-worth and bring more joy and fulfillment into your life.

EMBRACE THE HEALING JOURNEY

Life can sometimes throw us curveballs, but it's essential to remember that we have the power to heal and grow. So, let's embark on this journey together, and I'll share some thoughts with you.

It's crucial to decide what truly matters to you. Take a moment to reflect on your life, your values, and your dreams. What brings you joy? What makes your heart sing? These are the things that matter most. Your healing journey should align with your core values and aspirations.

Next, think about what you want to change and why it's so important to you. Perhaps it's a relationship that needs mending, a career shift, or personal habits you'd like to improve. Understanding the "why" behind your desire for change gives you a strong sense of purpose. It fuels your motivation and determination.

Kerri's Story

During an EMDR session, I encountered difficulties arriving at a meaningful revelation. My therapist sensed that I had not yet experienced a breakthrough and inquired if I wished to continue. I agreed to proceed.

The process involved repetition, frustration, and a surge of tears that made it challenging to maintain composure. Determined, we decided to make one more attempt, and suddenly, everything clicked into place.

In that pivotal moment, my thoughts shifted toward my great-grandmother, who is still with us today, and the unimaginable suffering she endured at the hands of her husband. I reflected on my grandmother's ordeal of abuse at the hands of her father and my mother's experiences of neglect. The pattern extended to the other side of my family as well—my dad, who had experienced both neglect and abuse and my granddad, who had endured his share of abuse.

This harrowing cycle had persisted for generations, spanning over a century. The weight of this realization was overwhelming. I came to understand that the resources and support available to me were starkly absent for them. Many of my family members struggled to secure even the most basic necessities, trapped in the throes of poverty.

The prospect of overcoming this deep-seated trauma appeared daunting, bordering on impossible. Historically, the stigma surrounding mental health has compounded the difficulty of finding a path to healing. Despite moments of frustration with those with the means and time for healing, a profound insight dawned on me during that session—I wielded control over my journey to healing.

As the session neared its conclusion, a powerful revelation took shape. It became clear to me that one of my life's callings is to break the cycle of generational trauma.

Now, here's the beautiful part: finding meaning and purpose in your healing journey. It's not just about fixing what's broken; it's about becoming the best version of yourself. As you embark on this path, you'll discover hidden strengths, resilience you never knew you had, and a deeper understanding of who you are.

THE INNER CHILD HEALING TIMELINE

I want you to know that patience and persistence are your best friends on this path. Healing your inner child is a deeply personal and unique journey. There's no one-size-fits-all timeline or fixed deadline for it. It's not like a race where you must reach the finish line by a certain date. It's more like a beautiful journey where each step you take is a victory.

Think of it like planting a seed and nurturing it into a thriving garden. You can't rush the growth of a plant. It needs time to put down roots, grow leaves, and eventually bear fruit. Similarly, your inner child needs time to heal, grow, and blossom.

Sometimes, it might feel like progress is slow or even non-existent. That's completely normal. There will be ups and downs, and that's okay. Just like a river, it has its twists and turns. These moments are opportunities for learning and growth, even if they don't feel like it at the time.

Your inner child might have wounds that run deep, and it takes time to unravel and heal them. But remember, every small step you take, every moment you spend understanding and nurturing your inner child, is a step closer to healing.

Be mindful of how you treat yourself along the way. Try to redirect that negative self-talk into personal compassion. You're doing the best you can, and that's truly admirable.

INTERACTIVE ELEMENT

Journaling Journey

It will be essential to continue your journaling journey as your inner child heals. This will help you learn and reflect as you go. Below are 10 journal prompts specific to inner child healing:

1. Who were your childhood role models or sources of inspiration?
2. Share a childhood memory where you unintentionally caused someone emotional distress. Can you recount the details?
3. Could you recall your earliest memory from childhood?
4. If you had the chance to send a message to your younger self through a letter, what would you want to convey?
5. Reflect on the most challenging aspect of your early years.
6. Recollect a moment from childhood when you felt a profound sense of lightness and carefree joy.
7. What was your preferred toy or pastime during your youth?
8. In your own words, what does the term "childlike" mean to you?
9. Can you think of something that used to frighten you when you were a child?
10. If you had to sum up your childhood in a single sentence, how would you describe it?

Self-Care Routines

Let's create a daily and monthly self-care routine to nurture and heal your inner child.

Daily self-care routine:

- **Morning mindfulness:** Start your day with a few moments of mindfulness. Find a quiet spot, close your eyes, take deep breaths, and focus on the present moment. Let go of any worries and embrace a sense of calm.
- **Positive affirmations:** Practice positive affirmations to boost your self-esteem. Tell yourself things like, "I am loved," "I am enough," and "I am deserving of happiness."
- **Journaling:** Dedicate a few minutes to journaling each morning. Write down your thoughts, feelings, and any dreams you remember. This helps you process emotions and gain insights into your inner child's needs.
- **Physical activity:** Engage in some form of physical activity you enjoy, whether it's a morning walk, yoga, or dancing. Exercise releases endorphins, making you feel happier and more connected to your body.
- **Creative expression:** Embrace your inner child's creativity. Draw, paint, write, or engage in any artistic activity that brings you joy and helps you express your emotions.
- **Healthy nutrition:** Nourish your body with wholesome, nutritious meals. Eating well-balanced food can positively impact your mood and energy levels.
- **Setting boundaries:** Practice setting healthy boundaries with others. This helps protect your inner child from unnecessary stress and discomfort.

- **Self-compassion breaks:** Throughout the day, take short breaks to offer yourself kind words and self-compassion. Be as gentle with yourself as you would with a child.
- **Evening self-care:** Wind down your day with a relaxing bedtime routine. This could include a warm bath, calming tea, or reading a soothing book.

Monthly self-care routine:

- **Inner child exploration:** Dedicate one day each month to deeply connect with your inner child. Reflect on your past, childhood experiences, and any wounds needing healing. Journal about what comes up.
- **Therapy or support group:** Consider joining a therapy group or support group where you can share your experiences and receive guidance on healing your inner child.
- **Nature retreat:** Plan a monthly nature retreat. Spend time outdoors, whether it's hiking in the woods, lounging on the beach, or simply sitting in a park. Being out in nature has a way of calming our souls.
- **Creative workshop:** Attend a creative workshop or class. This can help you tap into your inner child's creativity and provide an opportunity for self-expression.
- **Acts of kindness:** Engage in acts of kindness toward yourself and others. This can include volunteering, helping a friend, or pampering yourself with a spa day.

- **Self-care check-in:** Take a day each month to reassess your self-care routine. Are there any adjustments needed? Are you giving yourself the love and attention you deserve?
- **Forgiveness practice:** Dedicate time to forgive yourself and others for any past hurts. Be mindful that forgiveness can be a powerful tool when healing your inner child.
- **Gratitude ritual:** Create a gratitude ritual where you write down things you're thankful for in your life. This helps you focus on the positive and cultivates a sense of abundance.

As we conclude this chapter on the transformative art of reparenting our inner child, I want you to take a moment to acknowledge the incredible progress you've already made on your journey of self-discovery and healing. You've explored the depths of your past, nurturing the wounded parts of yourself with love, compassion, and understanding, and that is not easy.

The next chapter will explore the intricate web of resistance and self-sabotage, helping you understand why, at times, you may find yourself taking steps backward despite your best intentions. We'll unravel the complexities together, shedding light on the path to greater self-awareness and guiding you toward lasting transformation and inner peace. You're doing remarkable work, and I believe in your capacity to overcome any obstacles that lie ahead. Keep that loving inner parent close, for it will be your guiding light through the twists and turns of your journey.

4

RESISTANCE AND SELF-SABOTAGE

Healing takes courage, and we all have courage, even if we have to dig a little to find it.

— TORI AMOS

It's time to roll up our sleeves and dive deep into the process of healing that wounded inner child within us. It's a voyage filled with hope, compassion, and the promise of a brighter, more empowered future. So, let's get ready to reconnect with that inner child and offer the love, care, and nurturing they've been longing for.

Let's start with something important: unintentional self-sabotage. Change can be scary, even when it's a change for the better. Your inner child might resist healing because it's comfortable with the familiar, even if that familiar is pain. You might catch yourself making excuses or avoiding the work needed to heal. That's okay, too. Recognizing self-sabotage is the first step to overcoming it. Ask yourself, "Am I holding back because I'm scared of what lies ahead?" Remember, it's okay to be afraid, but don't let fear hold you back from the healing you deserve.

Another challenge you might face is the reactions of others. People around you, even well-meaning friends and family, might resist your changes. They may be used to the "old" you and not understand your need for healing. This can be tough to handle, but remember that this is about you, not them. You can't control how others react, but you can control how you respond. Keep reminding yourself of your worth and the importance of your healing journey.

Ask yourself, are you willing to let the opinions and reactions of others hinder your progress and happiness?

MAKING THE UNCONSCIOUS CONSCIOUS

Have you ever wondered why you react the way you do in certain situations or why certain patterns seem to repeat in your life? Well, a significant part of the answer lies in our subconscious mind. Our subconscious is like a vast reservoir of memories, beliefs, and experiences we've collected since childhood. These experiences have shaped how we view ourselves and the world.

Think about it for a moment: Those early experiences with our caregivers, peers, and environment play a significant role in forming our beliefs about love, worthiness, and safety. These beliefs, often buried deep in our subconscious, continue to influence our thoughts, emotions, and behaviors as adults.

So, why is it essential to make the unconscious conscious? Well, it's because we can't heal what we don't acknowledge. By bringing these hidden beliefs and memories to the surface, we gain the power to transform them. We can rewrite the stories we tell ourselves about who we are and what we deserve. It's like shining a light into the dark corners of your mind to reveal the cobwebs that have been holding you back.

Now, let's talk about how the subconscious works. Our subconscious operates by certain rules, and it's vital we understand them to work effectively on healing. It doesn't distinguish between past and present, and it doesn't judge or question the information it receives. It simply accepts and acts upon the beliefs and memories stored within it.

Imagine your subconscious as a loyal but somewhat outdated computer program. It's been running in the background, following the instructions it received when you were a child. It doesn't know that some of those instructions might be outdated, unhelpful, or even harmful.

So, the question becomes: How can we avoid the dangers of recreating memories and perpetuating negative patterns? Well, we can become aware of our thoughts and behaviors. Start asking yourself why you react the way you do in certain situations. Why do you have specific fears, insecurities, or limiting beliefs?

Challenge those beliefs and question their validity. Are they based on your current reality, or are they relics from the past? By shining a light on these patterns and consciously choosing to change them, you can break free from the cycle of recreating painful memories.

TYPES OF CHALLENGES TO BE PREPARED FOR

Have you wondered what challenges you might face along the way? If you examine them, you can be prepared and resilient.

The journey of healing often involves revisiting painful memories. As you delve into your past, it's natural for trauma and anxiety to resurface. This can be tough, but remember, you are stronger than you think. When these emotions emerge, take a deep breath, and remind yourself that you're safe in the present.

Sometimes, it might feel like your emotions are working against you. You might resist feeling certain things because they are uncomfortable or painful. But remember, healing means facing these emotions head-on. Embrace them, for they are a part of you, and they have valuable lessons to teach.

The inner critic and self-doubt—these can be like constant companions on your healing journey. They'll tell you you're not good enough and you don't deserve healing. But let me tell you something: you absolutely do deserve it. We'll explore strategies to deal with these inner naysayers in upcoming chapters, so keep moving forward.

Breaking free from negative parental patterns can be challenging. It might feel like you're betraying your family or doing something wrong. But remember, your journey to healing is about becoming the best version of yourself, not about hurting anyone else. We'll explore this topic extensively in upcoming chapters.

Setting boundaries can be tough, especially if you're used to putting others' needs before your own. But remember, establishing and enforcing your boundaries is a crucial part of self-care. We'll explore this in more detail in Chapter 11, so stay tuned.

It's not uncommon to feel guilty or have low self-worth when you start showing compassion to yourself. You might think, "Shouldn't I be tough on myself?" But self-compassion is the key to healing. Embrace it, and don't let guilt hold you back.

There will be moments when you feel like giving up or wonder if it's all worth it. During those times, ask yourself, "Am I willing to give up on becoming the best version of myself?" Keep your eyes on the long-term goal.

Opening up about your inner child's wounds and vulnerabilities can be scary. Fear of rejection might creep in. But remember, true connections are built on authenticity. Embrace your vulnerability, and you'll find that it can be a source of strength.

RECOGNIZING SELF-SABOTAGE AND WHAT TO DO ABOUT IT

Have you ever felt like you were on the verge of achieving something truly important, only to stumble and fall at the last hurdle? Maybe you've experienced the weight of stress and anxiety while pursuing a significant goal, leaving you frustrated, discouraged, and even angry with yourself. These emotions can create a suffocating cycle that prevents you from moving forward. Well, what you're experiencing is self-sabotage, and I'm here to help you recognize it and overcome it.

Self-sabotage is like an invisible hand that chips away at your self-confidence and self-esteem, affecting your personal goals and relationships with others. It can manifest in various ways, unique to each person, but there are common patterns we can recognize.

For instance, you might "forget" a critical deadline or botch a crucial presentation. Perhaps punctuality isn't your strong suit, or you have a knack for procrastinating despite knowing the urgency of a task. Maybe you're great at starting projects but struggle to finish them, or you dream of doing something truly significant but can't seem to take that first step. You might even find yourself inexplicably frozen when you should be charging ahead as if an invisible force is holding you back.

At the root of self-sabotage is often a negative internal dialogue. You might be telling yourself you're not good enough or don't deserve success. Thoughts like, "You can't do that!" or "If you try, you'll probably just fail anyway," can become the soundtrack to your life.

Now, it's essential to acknowledge that we've all danced with self-sabotage at some point, but some of us tango with it more frequently. The tricky part is recognizing when we're in the grip of self-sabotage because it can reinforce feelings of worthlessness and make those negative thoughts feel valid.

But here's the uplifting part: You can break free from self-sabotage and replace it with self-confidence. You can start this process with a few practical actions:

Action 1: Recognize Your Self-Sabotaging Behaviors

The first step toward overcoming self-sabotage is to identify your self-sabotaging behaviors. Think about the goals you've had for ages but haven't achieved. Are there areas where you consistently delay decisions or lack motivation, even for important matters? Take a moment to ponder what you habitually fail at, seemingly for no reason, and consider how it affects others around you.

I know it might be uncomfortable to ask yourself these questions, but it's essential to tune in to these situations so you can gain a deeper understanding of what's happening.

Action 2: Understand the Emotions That Lead to the Behavior

Self-sabotage often sprouts from emotions like anxiety, anger, and feelings of worthlessness. Let's say you left a report unfinished because your boss seemed distant, and it made you upset. Your emotional reaction led to a self-defeating action, even though your boss was likely preoccupied with other matters.

It's essential to learn to manage your emotions so they don't drive you toward negative behaviors. Keep an eye out for signs of anger and anxiety before they escalate.

Action 3: Spot the Thinking or Beliefs That Cause the Emotion

The emotions triggering self-sabotaging behavior often originate from irrational thoughts. In our example, you may tell yourself, "I'm such a failure; my boss has probably had enough of me!" But remember, your boss might have had other things on their mind.

When you find yourself engaging in self-sabotaging behavior, monitor your "stream of consciousness" and jot down all those negative thoughts in your journal, no matter how unrealistic they may seem.

Action 4: Change Your Behaviors, Emotions, and Thoughts

As you become aware of the emotions, behaviors, and thoughts fueling self-sabotage, it's time to challenge them. Changing just one of these aspects can make it easier to change the others, too.

Action 5: Develop Self-Supporting Behaviors

Now, let's rebuild that self-esteem of yours. Ask yourself positive and encouraging questions like:

- What can I say to myself that's uplifting?
- Are there multiple ways to achieve my goal?
- How can I boost my confidence by accomplishing smaller tasks on the way to bigger ones?

Use your answers to craft a motivating message. For example, "Even though I may not complete this project on time, I know I have the skills to get through it. When I start, I'll release the stress and anxiety I've been carrying." Write these messages in your journal so you can reflect back on them.

INTERACTIVE ELEMENT

Self-Sabotaging Behaviors Checklist

I would like to begin by encouraging you to create a checklist of self-sabotaging behaviors and find alternative choices to nurture that inner child within you.

Negative self-talk: Do you constantly criticize and belittle yourself?

- Alternative: Practice self-compassion. Replace those negative thoughts with positive affirmations. Treat yourself with kindness and love.

Procrastination: Are you putting off important tasks and goals?

- Alternative: Break tasks into smaller, manageable steps. Prioritize and take small actions each day to build momentum.

Perfectionism: Do you strive for impossible perfection?

- Alternative: Embrace imperfection. Understand that making mistakes is a natural part of growth. Aim for progress, not perfection.

People-pleasing: Are you constantly seeking approval and validation from others?

- Alternative: Focus on your needs and values. Say no when necessary and honor your boundaries.

Avoidance: Are you avoiding confronting past traumas or uncomfortable emotions?

- Alternative: Seek professional help if needed. Acknowledge your feelings and work through them, allowing healing to occur.

Comparison: Do you often compare yourself to others, leading to feelings of inadequacy?

- Alternative: Celebrate your uniqueness. Recognize that everyone's journey is different, and you are exactly where you need to be.

Self-Isolation: Are you withdrawing from social connections?

- Alternative: Reach out to friends and loved ones for support. Human connections are vital for healing.

Mindless consumption: Are you using distractions like excessive TV, social media, or substances to numb your pain?

- Alternative: Engage in mindful activities like meditation, journaling, or hobbies that promote self-awareness and growth.

Self-neglect: Are you neglecting self-care in terms of physical health, nutrition, and rest?

- Alternative: Prioritize self-care rituals that nourish your body and soul. Treat yourself with love and respect.

Fear of success: Are you afraid to step into your full potential?

- Alternative: Embrace your strengths and accomplishments. Visualize success and trust in your abilities.

Now, let's continue journaling, shall we?

- **Journaling prompt:** Reflect on one self-sabotaging behavior from the checklist that resonates with you the most. Write about a specific situation where this behavior has held you back in the past. Then, explore the alternative choices you can make to overcome it. How will making this change positively impact your inner child's healing journey?

As we transition into Part Two of this book, your healing journey will continue with seven empowering steps that guide you through reconnecting with and nurturing your inner child. Together, we will embark on this path of self-discovery, compassion, and growth that will not only mend the wounds of the past but also empower you to create a brighter, more deserving future.

PART II

LET THE HEALING BEGIN

5

STEP ONE—RECONNECT WITH YOUR INNER CHILD

Whatever is rejected from the self appears in the world as an event.

— CARL GUSTAV JUNG

Y ou might have noticed that lately, everyone seems to be talking about their inner child. It's all-over social media, especially on TikTok. People are sharing their experiences, engaging in healing activities, and even having conversations with their younger selves. But you might be wondering, what's all the buzz about, and why should you care?

Well, let me tell you, this concept isn't new at all. In fact, it goes back about a hundred years when the famous psychologist Carl Jung introduced it to the world. He believed that our inner child, the part of us that holds onto the emotions and experiences of our youth, plays a crucial role in shaping our adult lives (Haupt, 2023).

As you explore this topic, you'll gradually become more aware of your inner child's presence within you. And remember, it's okay to be gentle and patient with yourself during this process. Your inner child deserves love and care, just like any other part of you.

We'll delve deeper into inner child healing techniques, how to nurture your inner child, and the incredible transformations that can result from this practice. But for now, just take that first step of recognition.

MICHELLE'S STORY

Once upon a time, there was a woman much like you and me. Her name was Michelle. She held a stable job and appeared well put-together on the outside, yet beneath this facade lay a profound struggle—the enduring aftermath of a troubled childhood. This story commences when she was just seven years old, an age that should overflow with wonder and security.

At that tender age, her life took an abrupt turn. Michelle's parents, who should have been the source of love and solace, began to mistreat each other, creating an atmosphere of emotional detachment that extended to their children. Those once-affectionate parents transformed into distant figures, residing in separate rooms, engrossed in the glowing screens of televisions or the pages of books. Days passed without words exchanged.

Can you envision returning home from school, brimming with excitement to share your day, only to be met with cold, vacant gazes? It's a soul-aching loneliness. Over time, Michelle felt as though she was slowly fading into obscurity—did she even exist anymore? Loneliness became her daily reality, a part of her very being.

By the time she reached eleven years old, Michelle had mastered the art of being an adult in a child's body. She prepared her meals, tended to her hygiene, excelled academically, and even assumed the role of a caregiver for her mother and younger sibling. She wore the label of the "perfect child" with pride, earning accolades from teachers, family, and society for her maturity. However, beneath the surface, forming genuine connections with others remained an elusive challenge. It felt as though she lived in a world encircled by impenetrable concrete walls—always observing others, yet never truly connecting.

Anxiety became Michelle's constant companion, echoing the worries of a homeless child. Would there be enough food today? How would she reach school if she missed the bus? What if illness struck? Where would she sleep if locked out? What if someone inflicted harm?

As an adult, Michelle received a diagnosis of generalized anxiety disorder and came to understand that her anxiety was rooted in her childhood neglect. To cope as a child, she had developed survival strategies—pursuing perfection, staying invisible, and hoarding essentials. These tactics had ensured her survival in the past but now stood in the way of personal growth.

Striving for perfection meant avoiding any mistakes at all costs. Michelle wished she had stood up to bullies, but her parents' authority held a more terrifying grip. Staying invisible required freezing her body and emotions. This constant tension led to headaches, muscle aches, and ulcers. Hoarding food and medication became a necessity, driven by an ever-present fear of the worst, and she concealed her emotions behind a stoic demeanor.

Michelle's parents seldom displayed emotions, and when they did, it was unpredictable and unsafe. Her happiness or excitement often provoked irritation and disappointment from her father, casting a shadow over her joy.

However, as Michelle entered adulthood, she came to realize that the very survival mechanisms that once shielded her were now the sources of her anxiety. How could she break free from these deeply ingrained instincts? How could she reshape the person she had always been?

Michelle's journey to healing encompassed therapy and self-defense training. Through EMDR therapy and IMPACT self-defense, she embarked on the path of self-nurturing, offering her inner child a second chance at being cared for. The key difference: She became both the parent and the child. It all began with reconnecting to the neglected child within.

BENEFITS OF RECONNECTING WITH YOUR INNER CHILD

Reconnecting with your inner child allows you to tap into those pure, unfiltered aspects of yourself that you might have buried under the responsibilities and stresses of adulthood. When you embrace your inner child, you can better understand your true desires, passions, and values. It's like rediscovering an old friend—you might be surprised by how much you've missed them!

Now, what about the profound healing potential? Reconnecting with your inner child can be an incredibly powerful tool for healing past wounds and traumas. Through self-compassion and self-acceptance, you can provide the nurturing and love that your inner child may have missed out on. This inner healing can lead to a more balanced and resilient emotional state, helping you navigate life's challenges with greater ease.

Next up is enhanced creativity and playfulness. Remember how effortlessly creative and playful you were as a child? Reconnecting with that part of yourself can unlock a wellspring of creativity you might not have realized was there. It can make your daily life more enjoyable, infusing it with a sense of wonder and curiosity. You'll find joy in simple things, like drawing, dancing, or simply daydreaming.

Speaking of joy, that's another fantastic benefit. Reconnecting with your inner child can bring back that childlike sense of wonder and enthusiasm for life. You'll start to notice the small, beautiful moments that may have passed you by before. It's like seeing the world with fresh eyes, and it can bring immense happiness.

So, in a nutshell, rediscovering your inner child is a journey toward self-awareness, healing, creativity, and joy. It's like giving yourself permission to be your authentic, playful, and joyful self.

SIGNS YOU ARE DISCONNECTED FROM YOUR INNER CHILD

I would like to take a moment and discuss the signs that might indicate you're disconnected from your inner child, as well as the reasons behind it.

Identifying emotional and behavioral indicators of a weakened connection:

- **Emotional numbness:** If you often feel emotionally distant, like you're just going through the motions without really feeling joy or sadness, it might be a sign of disconnection from your inner child.
- **Difficulty setting boundaries:** Struggling to say no or constantly overextending yourself to please others can signal that you're not honoring your inner child's needs.
- **Perfectionism:** An unrelenting desire for perfection can stem from a lack of self-compassion and can be an indicator that you're suppressing your inner child's desire for playfulness and creativity.
- **Avoidance of vulnerability:** If you find it challenging to open up to others or express your true feelings, it

could be because you've buried those emotions deep inside.

Understanding the impact of stress, responsibilities, and societal expectations on disconnecting from your inner child is important.

Life can get hectic, and we often find ourselves buried under stress, responsibilities, and societal expectations. These external pressures can lead to a disconnect from our inner child in several ways:

- **Prioritizing adult responsibilities:** We get so caught up in our adult roles—work, bills, and obligations—that we forget to nurture our inner child's need for fun and play.
- **Fear of judgment:** Society can be critical, making us feel like we need to conform to certain standards. This fear of judgment can cause us to stifle our inner child's desires and authenticity. When was the last time you blew bubbles? Exactly, society would look at us, wondering why a full-grown adult is enjoying such an activity. Don't fear getting back to those childhood and creative activities; they soothe our inner child's soul.
- **Neglecting self-care:** When we're busy taking care of everyone and everything else, we often neglect taking care of ourselves. This neglect can lead to emotional detachment from our inner child.

Subtle ways in which you might have suppressed or ignored your inner child's needs:

- **Ignoring hobbies:** Have you stopped doing things you once loved? Maybe it's painting, dancing, or playing a musical instrument. Reconnecting with these hobbies can help you heal your inner child.
- **Neglecting self-compassion:** We often beat ourselves up over mistakes. Practicing self-compassion is like offering a soothing balm to your inner child.
- **Avoiding playfulness:** Do you avoid spontaneous moments of joy? Embracing your inner child means allowing yourself to be silly and playful from time to time. Jump on that trampoline! Do a cannonball into the swimming pool! Draw pictures with sidewalk chalk!
- **Not listening to your intuition:** Your inner child often communicates through your intuition. Ignoring it can lead to feelings of disconnection.

Remember, healing your inner child is a journey, and it's never too late to start. Begin by acknowledging these signs, being gentle with yourself, and taking small steps to reconnect.

HOW TO RECONNECT WITH YOUR INNER CHILD

I'm here to offer you some gentle guidance on reconnecting with your inner child. It's a beautiful journey of self-discovery and healing, and I'm excited to help you along the way.

Building trust with your inner child is key. Imagine your inner child as a vulnerable little you who needs love and reassurance. Create a safe mental space by visualizing a cozy room or a beautiful garden where you can meet and talk to your inner child. This space is free from judgment and full of warmth.

Embrace your inner child's sense of play and creativity. Engage in artistic activities like drawing, painting, or crafting. These activities can tap into your inner child's creativity, allowing emotions to flow freely. You don't have to be a professional artist; the process matters more than the outcome.

Incorporate playful activities like dancing, singing, or blowing those bubbles into your routine. These activities can release emotional blockages and foster a deeper connection with your inner child. Remember, it's about having fun and letting go of inhibitions.

Practicing mindfulness techniques can help you become more attuned to your present emotions and sensations. Connecting to your inner child this way is beyond powerful. Try this:

1. Find a quiet space and sit comfortably.
2. Close your eyes while taking deep, slow breaths.
3. Imagine yourself as a child, feeling safe and loved.
4. Ask your inner child how they are feeling.
5. Listen attentively to any emotions or memories that surface.

Guided meditations specifically designed for inner child work can also be beneficial. Incorporate mindfulness into your daily life to prevent future disconnection and maintain a strong bond with your inner child.

You are embarking on a beautiful journey toward self-love and healing, and I'm here to support you every step of the way. Keep nurturing that precious connection with your inner child, and you'll discover a profound sense of healing and joy in your life.

INTERACTIVE ELEMENT

Let's start by finding a quiet and comfortable place. Sit or lie down, close your eyes, and take a deep breath, filling your lungs completely. Exhale slowly, releasing any tension you might be holding.

Inhale again, and as you exhale, allow your body to sink into relaxation. Feel the support beneath you and let go of any worries or distractions for this moment.

Imagine yourself in a peaceful place, perhaps a serene meadow, a cozy room, or even your favorite childhood spot. Visualize this place in as much detail as you can. What colors do you see? What does it smell like? Are there any sounds, like birds singing or gentle music? When I do this exercise, I always put myself back in my grandmother's kitchen baking cookies. I smell her perfume and the chewy cookies. I can see her stained apron. I can hear her robust laughter. What is your safe, peaceful place?

Now, shift your focus to your inner child. Picture her as vividly as you can. Notice her appearance, her smile, and the way she moves. What emotions do you see in her eyes?

Take a moment to connect with your inner child. Approach her gently and tell her you are here to listen and understand. Ask her how she's feeling, what she needs, and what she'd like to share with you.

Listen to her carefully and offer reassurance. Tell her that you love and accept her just as she is. Embrace her with warmth and compassion, assuring her that you're here to protect and support her.

Now, let's slowly transition back to the present moment. Take a few deep breaths, and as you exhale, visualize your inner child merging with your current self, bringing her warmth, wisdom, and innocence into your life.

When you're ready, gently open your eyes and return to the present, carrying the love and connection with your inner child with you.

Inner Child Connection Exercises

It is vital we stay connected to our inner child. Don't forget to take care of yourself while doing so. I would like to share some exercises to do just that:

- **Childhood photo talk:** Place a photo of your younger self where you can see it daily. Take a moment each day to greet your inner child in the photo and say what she needs to hear. It might be words of encouragement, love, or comfort. It may sound something like this: "I am here for you unconditionally. I will protect you, and you can trust me."

- **Acknowledge your inner child:** Throughout the day, remind yourself of your inner child's presence. Whenever you face challenges or difficult emotions, acknowledge her and offer support.

- **Daily self-hug:** Embrace yourself in a daily self-hug, visualizing it as a loving gesture to your inner child. This simple act can provide a sense of security and care.

- **Happy childhood memory:** Take time to recall a joyful childhood memory. Visualize it in detail, savoring the positive feelings it brings. Many of us come from traumatic or toxic childhoods, and you may feel there was no joy for you then. Don't be afraid to focus on even the smallest of things. Your favorite blanket as a child, that one time your best friend shared a cupcake, or waking up to a fresh layer of snow on Christmas morning.

- **Mirror work:** Stand in front of a mirror and look into your eyes. Talk to yourself kindly, as if you were speaking to your inner child. Offer words of love, encouragement, and acceptance.

- **Letter to your inner child:** This is a big one. Try writing a heartfelt letter to your inner child, expressing your love, understanding, and support. Remind her that you are there for her. Take your time with this. For example, you could write, "I know you were often scared, but I am now here to protect you, and we are safe."

- **Playtime:** Set aside moments for play and creativity in your daily life. Engage in activities that bring joy and spontaneity, like skipping rope, dancing, or baking your childhood favorites.

Journal Prompts

It is time to pull out that all-important journal or the customized journal pages you printed from:

InnerChild.LeighWHart.com

As you reflect through this interactive element, write what you are feeling. Please review these inner child journal prompts:

1. **Childhood reflection:** What was your childhood like? Describe it in as much detail as you can remember: the good, the bad, and the ugly.
2. **Childhood needs:** What did you need most as a child? Reflect on the emotional support, understanding, and care you required but didn't get.
3. **Impact of childhood play:** How did childhood play shape the person you've become as an adult? Consider the positive influences and skills you gained.
4. **Words to your younger self:** If you could go back in time, what advice or comforting words would you offer your younger self? Maybe you want to let them know that they will be okay. It could be something as simple as "You are worthy and loved."

5. **A day in your inner child's life:** Imagine a typical day in the life of your inner child. Describe her activities, feelings, and interactions.

6. **Neglected moments:** Recall a specific time when you felt your inner child was neglected or unheard. Ask yourself what emotions you associate with that memory.

7. **Mixed childhood experiences:** Were there periods in your childhood when things were sometimes good and sometimes challenging? Describe these mixed periods and their impact.

8. **Unresolved issues:** Are there any unresolved issues or past traumas from your childhood that you believe need addressing or healing?

9. **Things that bother you:** List five things that bother you in your current life or that you're carrying from your past. Maybe you have difficulty trusting others. Could you have issues with saying no?

10. **Letting go:** What do you wish you could let go of to create a healthier and happier relationship with your inner child?

As you move through these exercises, be gentle with yourself, and know that you have the power to nurture and heal that precious part of you.

In this chapter, we've embarked on Step 1: a nurturing journey to reconnect with our inner child, a vital step toward healing and self-discovery. We've explored the significance of this reconnection, uncovering the profound benefits it brings to our emotional well-being and personal growth.

As we move forward, we'll delve deeper into the layers of our inner child's experiences, understanding the hidden wounds that may have shaped our adult selves. In the next chapter, Step 2: Your Inner Child's Hidden Wounds, we'll compassionately explore the scars and vulnerabilities beneath the surface, empowering us to heal and nurture our inner child even further.

6

STEP TWO—HOW TO UNEARTH AND UNDERSTAND YOUR INNER CHILD'S HIDDEN WOUNDS

Stop treating your wound like it's something you imagined. If you see the wound is real, then you can heal it.

— LEIGH BARDUGO

Childhood and generational trauma are more common than you might think. As a matter of fact, it's a staggering statistic that nearly 3 in 4 children, which equates to a whopping 300 million children in the United States aged 2–4 years, regularly suffer physical punishment and psychological violence (*Child Maltreatment*, 2022). That's a sobering thought, isn't it? This isn't just about numbers, though. It's about the lived experiences of countless people who carry these scars into adulthood.

But here's the good news: You're not alone on this journey. I'm here to guide you with empathy, understanding, and practical strategies to help you heal and grow. As we move forward in this chapter and throughout the book, remember these key points:

- **Take it at your own pace:** Healing is not a race. It's a deeply personal journey, and it's perfectly okay to go at a pace that feels comfortable for you.
- **No comparisons:** Your journey is unique, and comparing it to others won't serve you well. Just because Judy in the office brags about all the progress she's making in therapy and you feel stuck does not mean you are not moving forward.
- **Embrace the pain and grief:** Healing often involves revisiting painful memories. It's okay to feel sadness, anger, or grief. Be gentle with yourself and allow these emotions to surface. There will be days you don't want to get out of bed. Other days will feel fresh and invigorating. This is all normal.
- **Stop or slow down if needed:** If it feels overwhelming, don't hesitate to pause, or take smaller steps. Your well-being is the top priority. I often remind myself that healing is often a lifelong journey and that taking breaks can refuel our souls.
- **Reflect:** Remember to reflect back on Chapter 5 as your emotional toolkit; it's great to keep in your back pocket.
- **Pause:** Throughout this journey, it's important to pause and reflect on your progress. Take every single small

win and do your happy dance. Did you wash your hair today? Enjoy that bowl of ice cream!

- **Seek help when necessary:** Healing can be challenging, and there's no shame in asking for support. Whether it's from friends, family, or a professional, don't hesitate to reach out. I always find a scheduled "friend date" with my bestie to unload!

In the pages that follow, we'll look into the roots of your inner child's wounds, and by the end of this chapter, you'll have a clearer understanding of why certain experiences have left you scarred. So, grab a cozy spot, a cup of tea, or coffee, and let's start this transformative journey together. Your inner child is ready for some long-overdue love and healing.

UNVEILING THE UNSEEN SCARS OF YOUR INNER CHILD

Let's start by talking about hidden wounds and why they matter so much.

Imagine your heart as a garden, a beautiful space filled with flowers, but underneath the soil, there are roots of pain and hurt. These roots are your hidden wounds. They can stem from childhood experiences, like feeling neglected, witnessing conflict, or facing trauma. These hidden wounds are the emotional baggage we carry from the past, and they can cast shadows on our emotional well-being.

Have you ever felt an unexplained sadness or anger that seemed to come out of nowhere? Those emotions might be connected to your hidden wounds. When we don't acknowledge and heal these wounds, they can continue to affect us, much like weeds choking the life out of your garden.

Here's a strategy to try: Take a moment to close your eyes and visualize your emotional garden. What do you see? Are there vibrant flowers or tangled, gnarled roots beneath the surface? This simple visualization can help you connect with your hidden wounds.

So, why is it important to uncover these wounds?

Well, it allows us to become more aware of ourselves. When we understand the roots of our feelings, behaviors, and reactions, we gain insight into why we are the way we are. This self-awareness is the cornerstone of personal growth and self-improvement.

You need to be mindful that hidden wounds often fester beneath the surface, impacting your emotional well-being. Addressing these wounds can be so healing. It's like tending to an old, unhealed physical injury—once you clean and treat it, the pain begins to subside.

Many of our adult behaviors and relationship dynamics are influenced by childhood wounds. Typically, those we have buried or tried to ignore. Uncovering them empowers us to break free from harmful patterns and make healthier choices in our lives.

It is important to realize that your past trauma and hidden scars can often strain your relationships with others. By addressing these wounds, you can communicate more effectively, trust more easily, and build deeper, more meaningful connections with those around you.

Chelsea's Story

Chelsea's early years in bustling Toronto were filled with adversity. Her mother's addiction and her father's abusive nature cast shadows over her childhood. As the only child in a poverty-stricken family, Chelsea faced constant instability, moving frequently to escape landlords.

One enduring symbol of her difficult upbringing was her aversion to canned spaghetti, a reminder of her family's hardships. Witnessing her parents' physical altercations left deep scars, leading Chelsea to replicate chaos in her adult relationships and career choices.

In her 50s, Chelsea yearned for a better life. She sought therapy to heal from her past and learned self-care. This journey led to her transformation, shedding the burdens of her upbringing. Toxic relationships lost their grip, and she found a fulfilling career.

Chelsea eventually discovered peace and happiness. Her story proves that healing, self-discovery, and transformation are possible no matter the scars of the past. It's a testament to human resilience, self-care, and therapy's power.

In the end, Chelsea's story reminds us that pursuing happiness and healing our unseen scars can lead to a brighter future. If you're considering addressing your childhood wounds, remember that you deserve a life free from their burdens.

How do unseen wounds from our childhood manifest in adult behaviors and relationships?

Let's explore how these wounds can manifest:

- **Trust issues:** If you grew up in an environment where trust was repeatedly broken, you might find it difficult to trust others as an adult. You may always be on guard, expecting people to let you down. This can make it challenging to form healthy, secure relationships.
- **Self-esteem:** Childhood wounds can erode your self-esteem. If you were consistently criticized or made to feel unworthy, you might struggle with self-doubt and a negative self-image as an adult. This can hinder your ability to assert yourself and pursue your goals.
- **Communication patterns:** The way you communicate in relationships can mirror what you witnessed at home. If you grew up in a household with conflict or a lack of healthy communication, you might struggle with expressing your feelings and needs effectively. I like to put it this way. Our first learning experience with how to love and function in relationships is from what we see as a child. If your parents were volatile or abusive, how would you know how to function in a normal relationship? How would you know how to communicate in a healthy way?
- **Avoidance of intimacy:** Childhood wounds can make you wary of intimacy. You might fear vulnerability and push people away to protect yourself from potential hurt, making it difficult to form deep connections.

- **Repetition of patterns:** Sometimes, people unconsciously seek relationships that replicate their childhood dynamics. For example, if you grew up with a controlling parent, you might be drawn to controlling partners without even realizing it. We are often victims of repeating those toxic generational patterns.

- **Coping mechanisms:** Childhood wounds often lead to the development of coping mechanisms. Some may turn to unhealthy behaviors like substance abuse or overeating to numb emotional pain.

- **Perfectionism:** If you were raised in an environment where perfection was expected, you might carry the burden of perfectionism into adulthood. This can lead to anxiety, burnout, and strained relationships due to unrealistic expectations. I know of many functioning adults who struggled for years to determine where their chronic anxiety stemmed from. After uncovering some unseen childhood wounds, it was revealed to be that expectation of perfection from one or both of their parents.

- **Difficulty expressing emotions:** Suppressing emotions may have been a coping mechanism in your childhood. As an adult, this can make it hard to express your feelings and connect with others emotionally. It can be terrifying to pour your heart out because you expect that person to react as those in your childhood did. If you were met with ridicule or shame, that is what you will expect in adult relationships.

Here's a strategy: Picture yourself unzipping that backpack filled with negative beliefs and gently setting it down. Recognize that they aren't the truth. Visualize yourself taking them out, one by one, replacing them with affirmations of self-love and self-worth.

Your journey to unveil the unseen scars of your inner child is an act of self-love and self-discovery. Those hidden wounds may be affecting you more than you realize, but by bringing them into the light, you're taking the first step toward healing and personal growth.

EXPLORING THE ORIGINS OF HIDDEN WOUNDS

Childhood trauma can be likened to an old book we carry into adulthood, its pages filled with stories of our past. Imagine this book as a collection of chapters, each representing various experiences we encountered during our early years. These chapters could be moments of physical, emotional, or psychological pain stemming from family dynamics, life-changing events, or relationships that etched indelible marks on our hearts. We can be excited to flip to the next chapter, but at times, it can be difficult just to turn one page.

Consider this: Have you ever felt a wave of anxiety, sadness, or anger seemingly out of nowhere? It's like a storm suddenly brewing on a sunny day. These emotional tempests often have their roots in our childhood experiences.

One key to understanding hidden wounds is recognizing how suppressed memories and emotions can resurface. Think of it like a pressure cooker. When we bury our feelings and memories deep inside, the pressure builds over time. Eventually, it finds a way to escape, often in the form of unexplained emotional reactions, self-destructive behaviors, or physical symptoms.

Now, let's get into some unique strategies to help you navigate this complex terrain.

- **Journaling as a time machine:** Grab a notebook, and let's embark on a journey into your past. Write down your earliest memories and the emotions associated with them. Use descriptive language to recall those moments vividly. This can help you uncover repressed memories and understand their impact on your life today.
- **Conversations that heal:** I mentioned earlier how therapeutic it can be to sit with a great friend and spill it. Having that one person you can feel safe with and know you won't be judged is life-changing. There have been times throughout my life that I have had to be my person, my support system, and you can too. I am not asking you to have conversations out loud with yourself, although I'm not opposed to this in the least, but feel free to write yourself a letter. Give it a try!
- **Artistic expression:** Sometimes, words aren't enough to express deep-seated emotions. Try painting, drawing, or any form of creative expression that resonates with you. It can be a powerful way to access and release hidden pain.

- **Mindful meditation:** I will be the first to admit that meditation isn't always easy. Give this a try. Picture yourself in a tranquil forest. While you meditate, imagine opening doors to various corners of your past. Approach these memories with gentle curiosity, letting any emotions rise to the surface without passing judgment. This practice can assist you in finding peace with your concealed wounds.
- **Seek professional guidance:** If your hidden wounds are too overwhelming, consider seeking professional help. Therapists and counselors can be that person you dump all of your emotions and thoughts on without fear of judgment or shame.

Remember, exploring the origins of hidden wounds takes time, patience, and care. You are not alone on this journey.

UNCOVERING HIDDEN WOUNDS THROUGH INNER CHILD WORK

Before we dive into this section, it's important to acknowledge that this process can be emotionally challenging and may bring up intense feelings and memories related to childhood trauma. If you have a history of trauma or emotional distress, please proceed with caution, and consider seeking guidance and support from a mental health professional. Taking care of your emotional well-being is of utmost importance, and it's okay to always prioritize your mental health.

Have you ever wondered why certain emotions, reactions, or fears seem to linger in your life, even when you can't pinpoint their source? It might be because of your inner child—the part of you that experienced childhood and holds onto those memories and emotions. Inner child work is a powerful healing process that can help you uncover these hidden wounds and create a nurturing space for healing.

Think of your mind as a forgotten storage unit filled with boxes. Among them lie unprocessed emotions and memories from your childhood, carefully stored away. These unseen wounds can cast shadows over your relationships, self-esteem, and overall well-being. The good news is that you possess the ability to carefully unpack these boxes, heal those wounds, and pave the way for a more enriching life.

Let's start by understanding how to establish a dialogue with your inner child. Think of your inner child as a younger version of yourself, perhaps 5 to 10 years old. This inner child still carries the emotions, fears, and needs from that time.

Tip 1: Visualization Exercise

Find a quiet, comfortable space and close your eyes. Imagine yourself in a peaceful, serene place, like a meadow or a beach. This needs to be a place where you feel calm and safe. Now, visualize your younger self approaching you. This is your inner child. Picture them as vividly as possible. What do they look like? How do they feel? Begin a conversation with them, asking about their feelings and needs. What does this inner child need from your adult self? Be patient and let the dialogue flow naturally.

Creating a safe space for your inner child to express their needs and wounds is vital. Just like you would comfort a scared child, you need to offer that same compassion and love to your inner child.

Tip 2: Letter Writing Exercise

Grab a pen and paper and write a heartfelt letter to your inner child. Imagine you're speaking directly to that younger version of yourself. Acknowledge their pain, fears, and needs—promise to be there for them and support their healing journey. This exercise can be incredibly cathartic and healing. This also doesn't need to be a one-time thing. If you feel yourself struggling with something as an adult, for example, anxiety, write a new letter. Remind your younger self that they don't need to be perfect. That perfect doesn't exist, and they are beautiful just as they are.

EXERCISES TO HELP PROCESS TRAUMA

I would like to explore five exercises that can help you process past trauma safely and at your own pace.

1. **Sensory exploration:** Engage in sensory exploration as a means of reconnecting with your past and understanding your emotions. Gather objects or scents that remind you of your childhood, such as a childhood

toy, a family recipe, or a familiar scent. Spend time with these sensory cues and allow yourself to recall memories and emotions associated with them. This exercise can help you process trauma by connecting with your past through your senses.

2. **Time capsule letter:** Create a time capsule letter to your younger self. Write a heartfelt letter expressing understanding, empathy, and support to the child you once were. Share your insights, lessons, and encouragement. Seal the letter in an envelope and set a future date to open it. This exercise not only allows you to express your feelings but also provides a symbolic way to acknowledge and heal past wounds.

3. **Guided imagery healing:** Engage in guided imagery exercises specifically designed to heal childhood trauma. You can find audio recordings or videos online that lead you through a soothing and healing journey. These sessions often include visualizations and affirmations to help you reframe and heal painful memories. Guided imagery can provide a safe and structured way to work through trauma at your own pace.

4. **Body mapping and release:** Our bodies often store trauma and emotions. Try body mapping to identify and release stored tension and emotions. Sit in a quiet space and focus on each part of your body, starting from your toes and moving upward. Pay attention to any areas where you feel tension, discomfort, or pain. As you identify these areas, visualize releasing the emotions associated with them. You can use gentle

movements, deep breathing, or even light massage to aid in this process.

5. **Collage therapy:** Create a collage that represents your healing journey and emotions related to your childhood trauma. Collect magazines, images, and words that resonate with your experiences and emotions. Arrange these items on a poster board or in a journal to express your feelings visually. Collage therapy allows you to tap into your subconscious mind and can provide insights and a sense of empowerment as you work through your trauma.

These exercises are meant to be done at your comfort level. It's essential to be patient with yourself and ask for help if needed. Healing from childhood trauma is a personal journey, and these exercises can be valuable tools on your path to recovery.

THERAPEUTIC TECHNIQUES AND PROFESSIONAL SUPPORT

Have you ever heard of EMDR, somatic experiencing, or art therapy? These are not just fancy terms; they're powerful tools that can help us access those hidden wounds we carry within. It's like shining a light on the dark corners of our hearts and minds.

EMDR stands for Eye Movement Desensitization and Reprocessing. It's a specialized form of psychotherapy developed by Francine Shapiro in the late 1980s. EMDR is primarily used to help individuals process and heal from traumatic experiences, but it has also been applied to other mental health issues, including anxiety, depression, and phobias (*What Is EMDR?*, 2022).

Here's how EMDR therapy typically works:

- **Assessment:** The process begins with a thorough assessment by a trained EMDR therapist. During this phase, you and your therapist will discuss your history, symptoms, and the specific memories or experiences you want to target in therapy. It's important to establish a trusting therapeutic relationship during this stage.
- **Desensitization:** In the next phase, you'll focus on a specific traumatic memory or distressing experience. While recalling this memory, you'll engage in bilateral stimulation, which is often achieved through rapid eye movements, though other methods like tapping or auditory stimulation can also be used. This bilateral stimulation is thought to mimic the natural process of memory processing that occurs during REM (rapid eye movement) sleep.
- **Processing:** As the bilateral stimulation occurs, your therapist will guide you to explore your thoughts, emotions, and physical sensations related to the targeted memory. The goal is to help you process and reframe the memory so that it no longer triggers intense emotional distress. This phase involves a series of sets (usually around 20-30 seconds each) of bilateral stimulation while focusing on different aspects of the memory.

- **Reprocessing:** Over time, the distress associated with the memory should decrease, and you'll start to form more adaptive and less distressing beliefs about the traumatic event. Essentially, you're reprocessing the memory so that it's no longer as emotionally charged.
- **Integration:** The final phase of EMDR therapy involves integrating these new insights and beliefs into your everyday life. Your therapist will help you apply the changes you've made during the EMDR sessions to your current experiences and challenges.

One of the key ideas behind EMDR is that traumatic memories can become "stuck" in the brain, leading to emotional distress and symptoms like flashbacks, nightmares, and anxiety. EMDR aims to help unblock and reprocess these memories, so they no longer have such a strong hold on your mental and emotional well-being.

EMDR therapy has been extensively researched and has shown effectiveness in treating post-traumatic stress disorder (PTSD) and other trauma-related disorders. However, it's essential to work with a qualified and licensed EMDR therapist who has received specific training in this approach. If you're considering EMDR therapy, it's also a good idea to discuss it with your mental health professional to determine if it's the right fit for your specific needs and circumstances.

Somatic Experiencing (SE) is a therapeutic approach developed by Dr. Peter A. Levine to help individuals heal from the effects of trauma and stress. It focuses on the mind-body connection and recognizes that trauma is not just a mental or emotional experience but also a physical one (Levine, 2023).

In somatic experiencing (Levine, 2023):

- **Body awareness:** The therapist helps the individual become more aware of physical sensations and bodily responses associated with trauma or stress. This might include tension, pain, trembling, or other bodily sensations.
- **Titration:** SE is gentle and incremental, with a focus on pacing the therapeutic process to prevent overwhelming the individual. This allows the person to process traumatic experiences at a manageable rate.
- **Tracking sensations:** The therapist helps the individual track their bodily sensations, encouraging them to notice and explore physical sensations related to trauma without judgment.
- **Completing the stress response:** SE aims to help individuals complete the instinctual, biological stress responses that were interrupted during the traumatic event. This often involves facilitating the discharge of stored energy or tension in the body.
- **Resourcing:** The therapist helps the individual identify and develop internal and external resources to support their healing process, providing a sense of safety and support during the therapy.
- **Integration:** Ultimately, the goal of Somatic Experiencing is to integrate the traumatic experience into the person's life in a way that no longer disrupts

their well-being. This can lead to reduced symptoms and increased resilience.

Somatic Experiencing is often used to address various types of trauma, including physical, emotional, or psychological trauma. It is considered a holistic approach that recognizes the profound connection between the body and mind in the experience and resolution of trauma. As with any therapeutic approach, it's essential to work with a trained and licensed Somatic Experiencing therapist for the best results.

THOMAS' STORY

Thomas, like many men, grew up believing that showing emotions was a sign of weakness. So, he pushed his pain deep down, thinking he was strong for doing so. Growing up with a toxic mother and a father who abandoned them, he was taught men don't show emotions. You suck it up and tough it out.

But life has a funny way of teaching us lessons, and when Thomas became a father himself, he felt an overwhelming desire to break the cycle.

He wanted to be different for his children, to give them the love and support he never received. That's when he faced his unseen inner child wounds and sought help. It wasn't easy. The stigma around men in therapy weighed heavily on him, but he realized that strength wasn't about hiding his emotions; it was about confronting them.

With the guidance of a compassionate therapist, Thomas began the journey of healing. He started to unravel the tangled emotions he'd buried for so long. Through somatic experiencing, he learned to connect with his body's wisdom, understanding the physical manifestations of his pain.

Art therapy became his refuge, where he could express what words couldn't convey. Sculpting allowed him to give shape to his inner turmoil, making it tangible and manageable. EMDR helped him process traumatic memories, freeing him from their haunting grip.

So, what exactly is the role of a trained therapist?

Well, they are like skilled guides on this journey. They create a safe space for you to explore your unseen wounds, holding your hand as you face what's been buried.

Therapists are trained to ask the right questions to help you feel heard and seen. They use these therapeutic methods to assist you in unraveling the layers of pain, piece by piece. Imagine them as expert cartographers, helping you map your emotional landscape.

But why seek professional help when you could go it alone? Because it works. The benefits are profound. With the support of a therapist, you gain clarity, emotional resilience, and a deeper understanding of yourself. You learn how past wounds have influenced your thoughts, behaviors, and relationships. You discover that healing is not just about surviving; it's about thriving.

If you've been carrying hidden wounds like Thomas, know it's never too late to seek professional help. Embrace the power of therapeutic techniques and the guidance of trained therapists. It's a journey worth taking toward a life filled with healing, growth, and the freedom to be your authentic self.

INTERACTIVE ELEMENT

Danger Zone Checklist - When to Consider Therapy

It's a great practice to connect with yourself, and I'm here to assist you in crafting a checklist for recognizing when external support might be necessary. Life tends to present us with various challenges, and understanding when to seek help is a pivotal aspect of self-care.

Let's break this down into manageable portions, much like a trusted friend would:

For this task, I want you to create a danger zone checklist. This should include any triggers or reasons you need to seek help. Often, when we are in the thick of it, we don't see what we truly need. With this list, you can reflect on it and act.

Let's envision this scenario: You have a matter on your mind that's occupying a substantial portion of your thoughts. According to guidance from the American Psychological Association, contemplating therapy is worth considering when (GoodTherapy, 2022):

- there's a detrimental impact on your school, work, or relationships.
- the issue triggers embarrassment or a desire to avoid social interaction.
- it's affecting your overall quality of life or exacerbating it.
- you've started to make significant lifestyle changes or developed coping habits in response to the issue.
- devoting substantial daily time to thinking about or coping with the issue.

To put it in a relatable context, picture yourself trying to manage a hefty workload at your job, resulting in sleepless nights and anxiety. You've even started declining social invitations due to your preoccupation with work. This is a clear indicator that exploring therapy might be beneficial.

Sometimes, it's not just about the hours invested but the emotions that are creeping in. It could be the right time to reach out if you're experiencing:

- overwhelming stress, making it hard to catch your breath.
- unexplained fatigue or difficulty getting out of bed.
- unusually intense anger or lingering resentment.
- agoraphobia, which is a fear of specific places or situations.
- persistent anxious or intrusive thoughts consuming your mental space.

- a sense of apathy, where interests you once cherished have faded.
- overwhelming hopelessness or a belief that there's no future.
- a tendency to withdraw socially, even the mere thought of socializing causing distress.

Imagine yourself constantly on edge, struggling to focus on anything else due to racing thoughts. You're perpetually tired, and even the thought of spending time with friends feels like an insurmountable challenge. These signs are clear indications that it might be time to seek professional help.

"Calm Down Quick" Checklist

Now I would like you to make a "calm down quick" checklist. This tool can assist you in managing moments of intense emotions. Life can get hectic, and sometimes, we require a rapid method to regain composure. Here's a straightforward checklist to remember:

- **S = Stop:** Halt everything; press the pause button on your racing thoughts.
- **T = Take:** Take a few deep breaths to center yourself and fully engage with the present moment.
- **O = Observe:** Pay close attention to your inner state:

  ○ **Observe your body:** What physical sensations do you notice (touch, sight, hearing, taste, smell)?
  ○ **Acknowledge your emotions:** What are you feeling at

this very moment?

    ○ **Reflect on your thoughts:** What assumptions are you making about your feelings, and what stories are you telling yourself?

- **P = Proceed:** After this self-check, continue with intention. Return to your previous activities, but this time, incorporate what you've learned from your observations.

Visualize a heated argument with a loved one. Instead of allowing anger to dominate, utilize this checklist. Pause, take a breath, assess your racing heart and agitated thoughts, and then proceed with a more composed approach.

Always remember, it's perfectly okay to seek assistance when it's needed. Therapy can serve as a valuable tool for navigating life's complexities, and you don't have to tackle it alone. Numerous therapists are available, ready to accompany you on your journey toward a happier, healthier you.

Journal Prompts

1. What are your earliest memories from childhood? Go back as far as you can remember. What emotions do you associate with these memories?
2. Reflect on a specific life event that you believe may have wounded your inner child. Describe how it impacted you emotionally and how those feelings still resonate today.

3. Consider and write down any negative patterns you have developed because of that inner wound.

4. Explore any resistance or fears you may have about facing your inner child's wounds. What is one strategy can you use to overcome these obstacles and embrace the healing process?

5. Connect with a positive memory from your childhood that counteracts a hidden wound. Describe how revisiting this memory can bring healing and resilience.

6. Consider the role of self-compassion in healing hidden wounds. How can you cultivate a compassionate mindset towards yourself as you navigate this healing journey?

7. Envision the person you aspire to become after successfully addressing and healing your inner child's wounds. What steps from this chapter can you start applying today to move closer to this vision?

As we looked into the delicate landscape of our inner child's wounds with Step 2, we unveiled the tender parts of our past that still echo in our present. Recognizing these wounds is the first step toward healing. But remember, the journey toward wholeness is far from over; it's merely a shift in direction.

In the next chapter, Step 3 will have us explore how, armed with self-compassion and insight, we can become the nurturing parents we longed for in our childhood. It's time to lovingly guide our inner child in the direction of the healing and growth they've always deserved, stitching together the broken pieces with the thread of compassion and care.

7

STEP THREE—BEING THE PARENT YOU NEEDED BACK THEN

Reparenting is usually taught to parents because it's a way to care for yourself as an adult at the same time as caring for your children and to address your childhood trauma so you don't pass it on to your kids.

— VEX KING

In the pages that follow, the intent is clear: to introduce you to the profound practice of reparenting. It's a path that involves tending to your inner child, acknowledging those long-neglected emotional needs, and cultivating a sense of self-love and self-acceptance. We'll roll up our sleeves and engage in reflective exercises and nurturing self-care practices to help you uncover the beautiful tapestry of yourself.

As we progress together through this chapter, you'll gather the skills and insights essential for embarking on a transformative voyage of healing and self-empowerment. Isn't it fascinating that we all share this need to connect with our inner child, yet only a mere 20% of US adults actually take these vital steps (Terlizzi & Zablotsky, 2020)?

JUAN'S JOURNEY TO HEALING

Imagine a warm, sunlit park where vibrant flowers sway gently in the breeze. In the heart of this picturesque scene stands Juan, a man with a heavy heart and a troubled past. For years, he carried the weight of unresolved trauma like an anchor pulling him down.

One day, as he sat on a weathered bench, Juan decided it was time to confront the demons of his past. He began to explore the roots of his pain, recalling memories long buried beneath layers of defense mechanisms. He had to face the abuse suffered at the hands of an uncle. Years of emotional and physical pain were buried. It wasn't easy, but he knew it was necessary.

With the help of a therapist, Juan nurtured his inner child. He embraced the boy inside him, who had suffered silently for so long. Like a patient gardener tending to a fragile sapling, Juan watered his inner child with self-compassion and love. He forgave himself for the wounds he had endured.

Slowly, the clouds of his past began to dissipate. Juan's smile returned, brighter and more genuine than ever before. He rekindled his love for travel, filling his life with adventure. The park, once a place of sorrow, became his sanctuary of healing, where he found peace beneath the sun-dappled trees.

SOPHIA'S PATH TO RENEWAL

Picture a cozy coffee shop where the aroma of freshly brewed coffee mingles with the soft hum of conversation. Sophia, a young woman with a history of emotional pain, sat at a corner table, staring out of the window.

Sophia's past was like a storm that had raged through her life. Abandonment, neglect, and self-doubt had left scars that ran deep. But she refused to let those scars define her any longer.

One day, while sipping her latte, Sophia decided to embark on a journey of self-discovery. She started therapy, determined to confront the shadows that haunted her. It wasn't always easy, but she pressed on, unraveling the knots of her past piece by piece.

Through therapy, Sophia began to connect with her inner child —the little girl who had been hurt and frightened. She held that inner child close, comforting her with tenderness and understanding. As she nurtured her inner child, Sophia found the strength to let go of toxic relationships and self-destructive habits.

With each passing day, Sophia's eyes sparkled with a newfound sense of self-worth. She pursued her passions with vigor, rekindling her love for writing. Her once-dimmed light now shone brightly, illuminating the path to her dreams.

GOOD PARENTS VERSUS BAD PARENTS

What makes a good parent? A good parent is someone who provides love, support, and guidance to their children. They create a safe and nurturing environment where their kids can grow and develop both emotionally and physically. Good parents communicate openly with their children, listen to their needs, and encourage them to express themselves.

On the other hand, what constitutes a bad parent? Well, it's important to remember that nobody is perfect, and even well-intentioned parents can make mistakes. However, bad parents may consistently neglect their child's emotional or physical needs. They might be overly critical, abusive, or fail to provide a stable and loving home environment. Bad parents can also be those who are absent from their children's lives due to personal issues or addictions, leaving their kids feeling neglected and unsupported.

We need to remember that everyone's parents, even the good ones, will make mistakes. Parenting doesn't come with a manual, and we're all learning as we go. It's essential to recognize that sometimes parents have no idea what they're doing or are too wounded from their past experiences. In these cases, they may inadvertently harm their children without even realizing it.

Why do we need to let go of the past? It means accepting that your parents did the best they could at the level they were at during that time. This can be incredibly challenging, especially if you grew up in a toxic environment and your parents were at fault. However, letting go of blame and hurt is a healing tool for you, not an excuse for them.

The focus should ultimately be on what you need to move forward and heal. So, whether you had good parents, bad parents, or something in between, know that your experiences are valid, and you have the power to shape your life and future. It's about finding a path to healing and understanding.

THE POWER OF REPARENTING FOR SELF-HEALING

What exactly is reparenting? Reparenting means being your own loving and nurturing parent. It's like stepping in as the hero of your story and providing yourself with the emotional support, understanding, and love you might have missed out on as a child. Essentially, you're becoming the parent you needed back then.

Think of reparenting as a transformative self-care and healing practice. It's a way to address those emotional wounds and gaps from your past. By tending to your inner child's needs, you're not just healing old wounds; you're also fostering a deep sense of self-love and emotional resilience.

Now, why is this so important? Well, the relationship you have with yourself is at the core of your overall well-being. If you missed out on nurturing and support in your childhood, it could leave emotional scars that affect your adult life. Reparenting helps bridge those gaps, allowing you to heal and grow.

Reparenting isn't just about fixing what's broken; it's about nurturing what's already there. It's like planting seeds of self-love and self-compassion in the soil of your heart. As you water and care for these seeds, they grow into beautiful, resilient emotional landscapes within you.

Here's the incredible part: Reparenting is directly linked to your adult self-care practices. When you start treating yourself with the love and care you deserved as a child, it transforms how you approach self-care as an adult. You become more attuned to your needs, and you're more likely to engage in activities and habits that nourish your mind, body, and soul.

Reparenting is about showing yourself the love and care you might have missed out on in your early years. This practice can lead to a profound sense of self-love, emotional resilience, and personal growth. What we need to realize is that if we didn't get it as a child, we need to give it to ourselves as adults! You have the power within you to heal and nurture your inner child. Start today and watch how it transforms your life for the better.

RECONSTRUCTING AND REPARENTING

First, it's essential to decide what kind of parent you want to be to your inner child. Think about the qualities you wish your parents had provided when you were growing up. Perhaps it's love, understanding, patience, or even just a listening ear. Can you see that nurturing parent? Remind yourself you have the capacity to be that loving presence in your life.

I would like to talk about those old "tapes" that might be playing in your head from your parents. Many of us have them —those negative or critical voices that play in our heads over and over again. They could sound something like, "You will never amount to anything!" or "You are so stupid!"

It's now time to replace those tapes with a kinder, more loving, and compassionate voice. Your nurturing parental voice. When you notice that inner critic—those tapes playing—gently challenge it.

Ask yourself, "Would I say this to a child? Is this how I would speak to someone I love?" By doing this, you're gradually rewiring your thought patterns with positivity.

Embracing self-compassion is vital during this process. Remember that we aren't looking for perfection here, and mistakes are what make us human. Be patient with yourself, just as a good parent would be with their child.

Re-parenting isn't about erasing the past; it's about healing and growing from it. It's about acknowledging that you deserve love, care, and validation, and you have the power to give that to yourself. You are your greatest advocate, and by practicing these techniques, you can cultivate emotional resilience and inner strength.

INTERACTIVE ELEMENT

Releasing Those Heavy Emotions

First off, let's find a way to release those heavy emotions that have been weighing you down:

1. Sit or lie down in a quiet space where you can relax.
2. Close your eyes, take some deep breaths, and feel the rise and fall of your chest.
3. Think about an emotion you're holding onto from your childhood. It might be sadness, anger, regret, or anything else. Feel it, but don't get lost in it.
4. Now, imagine creating a box or bubble to put this emotion into. Picture it clearly in your mind.
5. Transfer that emotion into the container. You're doing great!
6. Gently, let this container float away into the universe. Feel the weight lifting off your shoulders as it goes.
7. Envision a comforting, healing light wrapping around you, warming and soothing your spirit.
8. Whisper to yourself some positive affirmations: "I am loved," "I am free," "I let go with grace."
9. When you're ready, open your eyes, and give yourself a big hug for taking this step. It's all about love and gratitude, right?

Rewriting Those Childhood Memories

Our past can shape us, but we can reshape our perspective on it:

1. Think about a childhood memory that seems to play on a loop in your mind, especially one that made you feel less than awesome. Remember those "tapes" we discussed?

2. Ensure the memory isn't too distressing. You should be taking care of your heart here.

3. Let's view this memory as if you're watching a movie, seeing your younger self from a distance.

4. As you watch, have an anchor ready, like focusing on your breathing or a nearby object. This way, you're grounded and safe. If you feel fear or anxiety creeping in, throw that anchor and feel it hit and sink into the ground.

5. Now, let's bring in a hero! Imagine someone you look up to, real or fictional, entering the scene. They're here to support and protect your younger self. Maybe this is your grandmother, your spouse, or Batman!

6. Watch as this situation changes, as this helper brings comfort, guidance, or even a change in the event's outcome.

7. When you feel complete, take a moment to appreciate this new story you've crafted. You've just given your younger self a gift of healing.

Embracing Your Inner Child

Let's connect with that wonderful, innocent inner child of yours:

1. Reflect on some childhood memories. They can be good, bad, or in-between.
2. Recognize the feelings your younger self had during those times. Continue to remind yourself that it's okay; you're safe now.
3. Give your inner child a voice. What do they want to say? How do they feel?
4. Acknowledge these emotions and let your inner child know that they are seen, heard, and deeply loved.

Journal Prompts

1. If you could say one thing to your parents or other adults in your life, what would it be?
2. What positive parenting qualities do you aspire to embody for yourself?
3. As you become the parent you need, how can you actively incorporate these parenting qualities into your daily life?
4. Examine the impact of parental figures on your self-perception. How have their words and actions shaped your beliefs about yourself?
5. How can you reshape these beliefs through reparenting?

6. Consider the interconnectedness of caring for yourself and others. How does reparenting serve as a tool not only for personal healing but also for breaking generational patterns of trauma within your family?

This chapter explored the powerful journey of becoming the parent we needed as children with Step 3. By acknowledging our past wounds and striving to provide the love, support, and understanding we longed for, we take a significant step toward healing ourselves and breaking the cycle of generational pain.

As we turn the page to the next chapter, we embark on a profound quest: the process of healing our emotional triggers with Step 4. It won't always be easy, but as we continue to nurture ourselves and foster compassion, we pave the way for a brighter, more resilient future. So, let's courageously step into the realm of emotional healing, armed with the love and care we've learned to give ourselves, ready to confront and conquer the triggers that have held us back for far too long.

THE IMPORTANCE OF TIME AND
SELF-COMPASSION

"Healing your lost inner child wounding takes time, gentle care, and learning to love and embrace your wounded parts."

— ROBERT JACKMAN

You're doing a lot of emotional work here, and I know it isn't always easy. It's important to take it at your own pace and take breaks when necessary.

Your inner child needs to be treated with kindness, and your adult self does, too. Take a moment to reflect on the work you've done so far and applaud yourself for having come this far. This kind of work takes courage, and although there's a stronger, more resilient you on the other side of this journey, your starting point was stronger than you might have realized. It takes strength to *want* to do this work, and that's a strength that you already have inside you.

As your healing process continues, you'll discover a sense of peace and fulfillment that might have evaded you in the past, and you'll realize how many more people could benefit from healing their inner child.

While we're taking a short break, I'd like to invite you to help me reach more people with the guidance they need to do exactly that. The great news is that this will only require a few minutes of your time, and compared to the effort you're investing in your healing journey, it's remarkably simple. All I ask is for you to share a brief review.

By leaving a review of this book, you'll help others find all the guidance they need to heal their inner child and step forward into a brighter, more confident future.

Your review will act as a guiding light, helping those already looking for this information to see exactly where they can find it.

Thank you so much for your support. The next step of your healing journey is waiting for you when you're ready.

Scan the QR code to leave your review.

8

STEP FOUR—HEALING EMOTIONAL TRIGGERS

If your emotional abilities aren't in hand, if you don't have self-awareness, if you are not able to manage your distressing emotions, if you can't have empathy and have effective relationships, then no matter how smart you are, you are not going to get very far.

— DANIEL GOLEMAN

In this chapter, we're going to shine a light on an imperative aspect of this process: healing your emotional triggers. You see, healing our past wounds and becoming more aware of how to navigate our emotions is like laying the foundation for a beautiful, sturdy house of personal growth. It's the kind of growth that doesn't just involve accumulating knowledge from books but also nurturing our emotional intelligence.

Did you know that only about 36% of people worldwide are considered emotionally intelligent (Costillo, 2023)? That's a staggering statistic, highlighting a vital need in our society. It's not just about academic learning; it's about understanding and managing our emotions, too. So, as we embark on this journey together, remember that you're not alone, and you're taking a significant step toward greater emotional wisdom and healing.

WHAT ARE EMOTIONS?

Think of your emotions as dishes you've savored over the years. Just like how you've had some unforgettable desserts or that one time you sent a meal back because it was awful, your emotions serve as your taste buds in the world of feelings. Their job? To help you refine your inner palate, to discern what's nourishing and what's not.

Now, these emotional dishes can sometimes be overwhelming, like a complex recipe that you're not quite sure how to follow. But here's the delicious breakdown:

- **Tasting the messages in every bite:** Emotions are like secret ingredients, revealing what's simmering within you—your heart, mind, and soul. They're your body's way of dishing out insights, and they come in all flavors —joy, sadness, anger, fear, and everything in between. Each emotion carries its own special recipe and message.
- **A chef's tasting menu of needs and attention:** When you savor these emotional dishes, it's a sign that

something needs attention in your inner kitchen. For instance, if you're savoring sadness, it might be because a part of you needs some tender care and affection. If anger is on your plate, it could be your inner child's way of protecting you from something or someone unsavory.

Emotions are like a culinary compass for your inner world. They're helping you discover the ingredients of self that could use a little culinary love, much like your inner child. They're whispering, "Hey, pay attention to this flavor! It's calling for some healing."

Now, it's perfectly natural to sometimes want to push away or hide certain emotions because they can be as challenging as cooking a complex dish. When you do that, it's like sending those friendly flavors back to the kitchen. Instead of closing the kitchen door, invite them in, savor their unique taste, and ask yourself, "What do I need right now? How can I create a more nourishing recipe for myself?"

So, the next time you taste an emotion stirring within, take a moment to savor it, breathe in the aroma, and explore its unique notes. What's that emotion trying to bring to your inner feast? How can you create a more fulfilling recipe for yourself? Emotions are your trusted sous chefs on this delightful self-discovery and healing culinary adventure.

HOW TO CULTIVATE EMOTIONAL AWARENESS AND MINDFULNESS

I want you to know something truly liberating and empowering: Your thoughts are not inevitable; they are entirely self-made. In fact, your thoughts significantly impact your emotions rather than the other way around. It's a simple yet profound truth that can change your life.

Reflect on a time you were really going through it, facing emotional hardships, and your mind was racing with all sorts of thoughts. Maybe it was self-doubt, worry, or negativity creeping in. That's when you can start taking control of your thinking.

I want you to become aware of the thought. Don't judge it; just acknowledge that it's there. Our thoughts pop up like uninvited guests sometimes, but that's okay. Next, ask yourself, "Is this thought healthy and beneficial for me?" This simple question can be so helpful.

If you find that the thought isn't doing you any good, don't fret. Take a deep breath and exhale slowly three times. As you do this, let a soft smile spread across your face. Imagine looking up at the vast, open sky and letting that thought go. It's as though you're exhaling it with every breath, gently releasing it.

Unlike when you were a child, you're in control here. Your mind is your domain, and you have the power to choose what you allow in. You have the power to shape your thoughts, and that, in turn, shapes how you feel. So, after releasing that unhelpful thought, pick a more uplifting one to replace it.

Choose a thought that better serves you and aligns with your emotional well-being.

This process might sound simple, but it's incredibly effective. Repeat it whenever unhelpful thoughts affect your emotions and even your physical well-being. Over time, you'll find that you're not just reacting to your thoughts but actively steering your emotional ship toward smoother waters.

WHAT CAN WE DO ABOUT UNWANTED OR UNHELPFUL EMOTIONS?

If you've felt the weight of a wounded inner child in your adult life, impacting your work and relationships, know that you are not alone. I've been there, and I understand how those negative emotions can erupt like a storm within you.

When those waves of negative emotions start crashing down, take a moment to be curious. What is the root cause? It could be a specific situation or even the way you're interpreting it. Maybe it's the relentless stress from work or how you perceive certain life events. Remember, your thoughts hold tremendous power over your emotions. Once you pinpoint the source, you're already on the path to finding relief.

Now that you've unlocked the mysteries of your inner child's wounds, it's time to take compassionate action. While you can't control everything, there are steps you can take to ease the burden of these emotions. Here's how:

- **Think of your workplace as a space of growth:** If it's causing stress, consider delegating tasks, setting boundaries, or seeking support. You don't have to carry the weight alone.
- **In your relationships, imagine yourself as a peacemaker:** Learning assertive communication can resolve conflicts and soothe emotional turmoil. Through cognitive restructuring, you can nurture positive thought patterns.
- **There may be things beyond your control:** You are going to have to learn to be okay with that. Dwelling on the unchangeable won't bring you peace. Focus your energy on what you can influence and watch your life flourish.

Sometimes, changing your external circumstances isn't enough. You'll also need loving outlets for those intense emotions. Think of these outlets as the nurturing embrace your inner child deserves.

Lastly, let's embrace the beautiful rainbow of your emotions, even the ones that don't feel so pleasant—fear, anger, sadness, or frustration. Instead of pushing them away, invite them in without judgment. This act of self-compassion is like giving your wounded inner child the love and permission to heal.

EMOTIONAL RELEASE: BUILDING A SAFE SPACE TO
PREVENT FURTHER REPRESSION

Have you ever wondered why we need an emotional release?
And if we need this release, why does it need to be done in a
safe space? Well, emotions are tricky little buggers on a good
day. If we are talking about negative emotions, they will sneak
back into the abyss at the smallest whiff of danger or insecurity.
You can be moving along in therapy and doing great, but the
second you encounter an emotion you feel uncomfortable with,
the walls go up, and you hear, "Danger, danger, get out!" When
we work through these situations in a safe space, we are far
more likely to not only deal with them but not try and stuff
them back into our pockets like delicious warm Pop-Tarts.

Repressing your emotions is like putting so many Pop-Tarts in
your pockets; you weigh yourself down, creating a heavy
burden, making it difficult for your inner child to breathe and
grow. By creating a safe space for emotional release, you ensure
that these buried emotions can surface and be processed,
preventing further repression.

Many of us carry old emotional wounds from our childhood
—Pop-Tarts— These wounds can fester (or go moldy) if left
unattended, affecting our present and future. By providing a
supportive environment for emotional release, you're giving
your inner child the opportunity to heal these wounds,
allowing you to move forward with greater emotional freedom.

Emotions that are suppressed or ignored can take a toll on your
mental and physical well-being. If your days are spent worrying

about the weight of those Pop-Tarts and if anyone else can see them, it will lead to stress, anxiety, and even physical ailments. Creating a nurturing space for emotional release can positively impact your overall health, allowing you to feel lighter and more at ease.

Unprocessed emotions can spill over into your relationships, causing misunderstandings and conflicts. By addressing and releasing these emotions in a supportive environment, you can improve your relationships with others and build deeper connections based on understanding and empathy.

When you create a safe space for emotional release, you empower yourself to take control of your emotional well-being. It's a journey of self-discovery, where you'll gain a deeper understanding of yourself and your inner child's needs and desires.

Repressed emotions often mask your true self. By allowing these emotions to surface and be processed, you can live more authentically, embracing your true nature and living a life that aligns with your values and desires.

Emotional release is not a sign of weakness; it's a display of resilience. It takes courage to face your emotions head-on. By doing so, you build emotional resilience that can serve you well in facing life's challenges.

So, how do we create a safe space for emotional release?

Find a quiet spot to just be. It could be a cozy chair at home, a park, or even your bed. The key is to find a place where you feel at ease and can let your guard down.

Sit up straight, but comfortably so. Your comfort is paramount because it allows you to focus on what truly matters.

Close your eyes and take a few moments to just be in the silence. You can choose to focus on your breath, the rise and fall of your chest, or even repeat a soothing mantra if that resonates with you.

Now, with your eyes still gently closed, let's explore a recent moment in your life that stirred up some strong emotions. Maybe it was a disagreement with a loved one, a situation where you felt mistreated, or an old wound that got reopened. Think about this incident as if you were telling a story to a friend, with vivid details.

At this moment, you are not the event. You are not the argument or the emotional upset. You are the calm observer, watching it all unfold from a place of serenity.

Now, let's name those emotions. What did you feel during that incident? Was it frustration, anger, sadness, or something else entirely? Be as specific as you can. Give that emotion a name and hold it gently in your awareness.

As we dive deeper, gently shift your focus away from that emotional word. Instead, turn your attention inward to your body. Emotions aren't just in your mind; they manifest physically, too. It's why we call them "feelings."

As you recall that incident, let your attention travel through your body. Notice where the memory stirs physical sensations. Perhaps it's a tightness in your chest, a knot in your stomach, or a lump in your throat. Locate where in your body you're holding onto this emotional experience.

Now, it's time to express it physically. Place your hand on the part of your body where you feel the sensation most strongly. Say it out loud, "It hurts here." If you sense the pain in multiple places, move your hand around and express the pain at each spot. It's about acknowledging these sensations and letting them be heard.

Another powerful way to express your emotions is through writing. Put pen to paper and let your feelings flow. Write about the painful experience in the first person (I/we), as if you're talking to yourself, then switch to the second person (you/they), addressing the situation, and finally, write it as if you're an impartial observer.

These feelings are yours. They are happening inside your body right now as you remember that moment. Even though the external event is in the past, your body is still reacting. It's not about blame or guilt; it's about understanding and taking responsibility for your feelings.

You have the power to respond to these emotions in new, creative ways. By taking responsibility, you're no longer dependent on others to make the pain go away. Hold onto this understanding for a few moments.

Now, let's release these emotions. Focus your attention on the part of your body where you're holding onto that pain, and with each exhale, intend to release the tension. Picture the painful sensation leaving your body with every breath out.

Some find making an audible sound that resonates in that area helpful.

Try different things to find what works best for you. Sing, dance, try deep breathing, or even use essential oils. Eating a couple of Pop-Tarts is not out of the question! If you've written down your emotions, consider a ritual: burn the paper and offer the ashes to the winds, symbolizing the release of those feelings.

You can use this exercise whenever you're upset to free yourself from emotional turmoil and the underlying pain. As you do, you'll find that opportunities for growth and healing will arise more frequently in all aspects of your life.

HOW TO VALIDATE AND NURTURE YOUR INNER CHILD'S EMOTIONS

While traveling the healing path of your inner child, you need to keep telling yourself that your emotions are real and valid, and acknowledging them is the first step in the direction of your best life. Your inner child might be hurting, and it's essential to provide comfort and reassurance. Here are some encouraging phrases your inner child needs to hear from you:

- **"What happened was not your fault."**: It's essential to remind yourself that the pain you carry wasn't something you caused. You were just a child, and you didn't have control over the circumstances.
- **"You are not alone."** Loneliness can exacerbate emotional wounds. Let your inner child know you're

there for them now, and they don't have to face their pain alone.

- **"You are worthy of getting your needs met."** Your needs are important, and they deserve to be met. Don't ever doubt your worthiness. You are deserving of love, care, and understanding.

- **"I love you just as you are."** Your inner child needs unconditional love. Embrace them with love and acceptance, flaws and all. You are enough just as you are.

- **"It's okay to express your feelings."** Encourage your inner child to express their emotions without judgment. Let them know that it's safe to feel and share their feelings.

- **"I'm here to protect and nurture you."** Be the protector your inner child needs. Show them that you're there to keep them safe and provide the care they missed out on.

- **"You have the power to heal."** Empower your inner child by letting them know that healing is possible. Together, you can work through the pain and find peace.

- **"You are strong and resilient."** Remind your inner child of their inner strength. They've survived so much, and that strength will aid in their healing journey.

- **"You are capable of change."** Change is a beautiful part of life. Assure your inner child that they can grow, adapt, and transform their pain into strength.

- **"You are enough just as you are."** Worthiness bears repeating. You are inherently valuable, and you don't need to prove your worth to anyone.

INTERACTIVE ELEMENT

For this element, I would like to talk about some tools and ideas that can help you manage emotional stress and anxiety, ultimately building resilience and emotional strength.

Creative Self-Expression

Engaging in creative activities can be incredibly therapeutic. It allows your inner child to express itself in a safe and creative way. Here's how you can incorporate this into your healing journey:

1. **Choose an outlet:** Select a creative outlet that resonates with you—it could be painting, drawing, writing, dancing, or even cooking.
2. **Set aside time:** Dedicate time regularly to engage in your chosen creative activity. This should be a time when you can freely express yourself without judgment.
3. **Let go of expectations:** Don't focus on the end result; focus on the process. Allow your inner child to play and explore without worrying about perfection.
4. **Reflect on your creations:** After your creative session, take a moment to reflect on what you've created. What emotions or memories came up during the process?

Floating Therapy

Float therapy, also known as sensory deprivation or flotation therapy, involves lying in a specially designed tank filled with water super-saturated with Epsom salt, allowing the individual to float effortlessly on the surface. The water and air are typically heated to skin temperature, making it difficult to distinguish between parts of the body that are in contact with the water and those that are not. When the tank is closed, it becomes dark and soundproof, removing visual, auditory, and most tactile stimuli. This environment creates a unique opportunity for deep relaxation and introspection.

Exploring Triggers Exercise and Journal Prompts

I would like you to reflect on the various things that can trigger your emotional reactions and behaviors. Grab your journal and identify two general types of situations that have triggered the behavior you wish to change. Then, explore the following categories:

1. **Emotional state:** Think about when you felt angry, depressed, happy, or sad. How did these emotions relate to the behavior?
2. **Physical state:** Consider times when you were relaxed, tense, tired, or aroused. How did your physical state contribute to the behavior?
3. **Presence of others:** Reflect on situations involving specific individuals. Were there certain people present when the behavior occurred?

4. **Availability:** Were there specific circumstances or resources available that triggered the behavior?
5. **Physical setting:** Contemplate where the behavior typically occurs. Is it at work, parties, your ex-spouse's house, or elsewhere?
6. **Social pressure:** Explore if you ever felt coerced or pressured into actions you didn't want to take. How did this influence your behavior?
7. **Activities:** Think about your engagement in different activities such as work, working at home, sports, watching TV, or playing cards. How did these activities relate to the behavior?
8. **Thoughts:** Recall times when certain thoughts influenced your behavior. How did your thoughts contribute to the behavior?

To better understand your triggers and the associated consequences, try the following while focusing on one high-risk trigger situation from your past:

- Briefly describe this situation and explore both its negative and positive consequences.
- Consider whether these consequences manifested immediately or were delayed.

This exercise encourages you to draw from your real-life experiences, promoting self-reflection and aiding in identifying triggers and their subsequent impacts on your behavior and emotions.

We've taken significant strides in identifying the emotional triggers influencing our thoughts, actions, and reactions with Step 4. This newfound self-awareness is a powerful tool for healing and growth. With a clearer understanding of what sets off our inner child's responses, we are now better equipped to address the challenges that lie ahead.

In the next chapter, with Step 5, we will explore how to transform negative self-talk, challenge invalidating beliefs, and break free from destructive patterns that have held us captive. By building on the insights gained here, we move closer to reclaiming our true selves and forging a path toward lasting healing and emotional well-being.

9

STEP FIVE—TRANSFORM NEGATIVE SELF-TALK

Either you must control your thoughts, or the outside forces will control them, and be warned that outside forces usually consist of fears, worries, and doubts.

— MADDY MALHOTRA

In this chapter, we're diving headfirst into the wonderful world of transforming negative self-talk, invalidating beliefs, and those pesky destructive patterns that seem to have a knack for holding us back. Now, I know what you might be thinking: "Oh no, not another chapter on this stuff!" But trust me, understanding and conquering these inner adversaries is like shining a light into the darkest corners of your mind.

We humans have a whopping 12,000 to 60,000 thoughts buzzing around in our heads each day. Shockingly, a whopping 80% of them are negative, and if that wasn't enough, a staggering 95% of those thoughts are just the same old, repetitive ones as the day before, with roughly 80% of them still clinging to that negative vibe (Simone, 2017). It's like Groundhog Day inside your mind, right? But fear not because together, we're going to break free from this cycle right from within your head!

WHAT IS NEGATIVE SELF-TALK

Negative self-talk occurs when the voice within you becomes overly critical, resembling an internal critic rather than a cheerleader. This mindset tends to be pessimistic, fixating on the negatives and undermining your self-assurance. As a result, it hampers your ability to tap into your full potential, often leading you to believe that failure is inevitable right from the get-go.

Negative self-talk is like having a tiny, annoying roommate living inside your head. This little voice often sneaks in, making snarky comments about your abilities, appearance, or worth. It's the one that says, "You're not good enough," "You can't do this," or "You'll never succeed."

Now, let's be real for a moment. We all have moments of self-doubt and self-criticism. It's normal. But when this negative chatter becomes a constant presence, it can seriously affect your self-esteem, relationships, and overall well-being.

Negative self-talk isn't just annoying; it's harmful. It can create a self-fulfilling prophecy. If you constantly tell yourself you'll fail, you might subconsciously sabotage your efforts. It can also lead to anxiety, depression, and a slew of other mental health issues.

It's essential to challenge these negative thoughts. We discussed earlier about asking, "Are they based on facts, or are they just old, outdated beliefs that need to be tossed out like yesterday's leftovers?

UNHELPFUL CORE BELIEFS

So, what are these pesky unhelpful core beliefs, you ask? Well, they're like those sneaky little gremlins hiding in the dark corners of your mind, whispering all sorts of negative nonsense about yourself. These beliefs are the stories we tell ourselves about who we are, and unfortunately, they tend to be more fiction than fact.

Let's shine a light on some common examples to give you a clearer picture:

- **I'm unlovable:** This belief convinces you that no one could ever truly love or care about you. It's like a broken record playing in your head, making you doubt the love and affection others offer.
- **I'm worthless:** This one tricks you into thinking you have no value, that your contributions don't matter, and that you're a burden to those around you. Spoiler alert: It's a blatant lie.

- **I'm unwanted:** This belief makes you feel like you're the last kid picked for the team, even when there's no team to be picked for. It convinces you that you're constantly on the outskirts of other people's lives.
- **I'm not allowed to defend myself:** This sneaky belief keeps you silent when you should speak up. It tells you that your voice doesn't matter, your opinions aren't valid, and you're better off staying quiet. Well, we're here to tell it to pipe down!

These beliefs are like uninvited guests at your inner child's tea party, and it's time to kick them out. They're unhelpful because they limit your potential, hinder your growth, and hold you back from living your best life.

OUR INNER CHILD'S HIDDEN BELIEFS AND BEHAVIORS AND HOW TO CHANGE THEM

Thoughts: They're a bit like the ever-changing weather. Sometimes sunny, other times stormy. The key is thoughts just happen; they're part and parcel of the human experience. Like taking a deep breath, we can also choose to steer our thoughts. But let's be real; our minds sometimes have a mind of their own, throwing thoughts our way uninvited. It's just part of being human, isn't it?

I've discovered that thoughts tend to settle down when we fully embrace the present moment. Picture feeling the sun's warmth on your skin or hearing birds chirping. Even the scent of wet dogs can do the trick! Moments of awe can work wonders, too.

So, keep an eye out for those awe-inspiring experiences, whether in nature or through art.

So, how do we usually treat our thoughts? We often treat them like rock-solid facts, such as "I'm a loser" or "I'll never find a job again." We've all been there, right? But the magic happens when we learn to watch our thoughts without getting tangled up in them.

Meditation can be your trusty sidekick in this adventure. When I began, I was clueless about meditation, too. My aim was to hush those noisy thoughts, especially the ones causing me grief. I'd focus on sensations like the wind on my skin or the scent in the air. It helped, but it didn't always silence the thoughts. And guess what? That's perfectly fine! Most meditation experts will tell you it's about observing, not stopping. Recognize those recurring patterns—fear, anger, worry, jealousy—and watch them drift by like clouds in the sky. They're just thoughts, not your entire reality.

Mornings can often become thought marathons for many of us. Random thoughts about breakfast or bills? Those early-morning mental races happen to the best of us. With time and practice, you'll get better at reining them in. Come back to the present, feel your breath, your body. Remind yourself that these thoughts are like passing clouds, not unshakable truths.

But let's be real; it's not about being a thought-watching guru 24/7. When life is comfy, it's easy to forget to observe your thoughts. Suddenly, you're in the shower, realizing you've been on autopilot for days. During tough times, I've found it's more effective to immerse myself in the moment, to be so present that thoughts can't steal the show. It's not about escaping; it's about "rising above thought," as Eckhart Tolle puts it (Tolle, 2023).

Don't take everything your thoughts say at face value. Repeat it like a mantra: "Don't believe your thoughts. Don't believe your thoughts. Don't believe your thoughts." Negative or painful emotions often tag along when we buy into our thoughts. "I messed up," "She's ignoring me," "I should be different." Sound familiar? Yeah, it's a slippery slope.

Think of your thoughts as storytellers. They craft tales about the past, the future, or the current situation. But they're not the same as being genuinely present. The truth is arguing with reality leads to more pain. So, peel the onion, my friend. Observe your thoughts, but don't get caught up in their drama. That's the secret sauce for inner peace.

But what about those sneaky beliefs that might be holding you back? These beliefs often stem from childhood, those moments when you absorbed messages like a sponge. Here are some potential burdens you're carrying:

- "You are my entire world."
- "You are my only reliable source."
- "I can't survive without you."
- "Nobody else cares about me except you."

And don't forget these classics:

- "There's something fundamentally wrong with you."
- "You're nothing but a disappointment."
- "No one cares about your thoughts."
- "You'll never amount to anything."

You can lighten your load by examining and replacing these beliefs with empowering ones. It's like giving your soul a good spring cleaning.

INTERACTIVE ELEMENT

Exercise: Discovering Your Core Beliefs

Let's roll up our sleeves and dive into understanding those beliefs that have been running the show in your mind. Remember, these beliefs are like stubborn guests at a party that just won't leave, but we're going to kindly show them the door.

Quickfire Belief Statements

Grab a pen and some paper. Don't overthink this; just let your thoughts flow. Complete the following sentences:

- I am_____
- Other people are_____
- The world is_____

It's like a mental snapshot of how you see yourself, others, and the big, wide world out there.

Take a moment to ponder those statements. How do they make you feel? Do they light you up like a Christmas tree, or do they feel like a heavy backpack you've been lugging around?

Think back to when you first became aware of these beliefs. Were they a gift from your childhood? Maybe they came from an experience that left its mark on you. Can you identify who in your life might share similar views?

Ask yourself, do these beliefs still serve me? Are they helping me become the best version of myself, or are they more outdated than a floppy disk?

Now, it's time to envision a brighter future. Write down three things you believe about yourself, other people, and the world that you'd like to foster going forward. These are like planting seeds for a beautiful mental garden:

- I am_____
- Other people are_____
- The world is_____

Think of these beliefs as your personal cheerleaders, always rooting for your success and happiness.

Journal Prompts

1. Reflect on a recent instance of negative self-talk. What triggered it, and how can you identify and challenge the underlying beliefs contributing to this negativity?
2. Examine an unhelpful core belief you hold about yourself. How did this belief originate, and what steps can you take to replace it with a more empowering and constructive belief?
3. Identify a recurring destructive pattern in your thoughts or actions. Can you trace its origin and how can you reframe this pattern to promote self-compassion and growth?
4. Explore a positive narrative or belief you want to cultivate. How does adopting this narrative contribute to your overall well-being, and what steps can you take to reinforce it?

As we wrap up Step 5 in this chapter on transforming negative self-talk, invalidating beliefs, and those sneaky destructive patterns, I want you to pat yourself on the back. You've taken a courageous step in the direction of healing your inner child.

Now, it's time to build upon this foundation as we venture into the next chapter with Step 6. Get ready to explore how establishing healthy boundaries is the key to maintaining your newfound self-worth and protecting the beautiful growth you're nurturing within.

10

STEP SIX—THE BOUNDARY LINE

You have to love and respect yourself enough to not let people use and abuse you. You have to set boundaries and keep them, let people clearly know how you won't tolerate to be treated, and let them know how you expect to be treated.

— JEANETTE CORON

O ur unique paths to healing our inner child mean that personal boundaries can differ greatly from one of us to the next. This underscores the significance of being explicit and communicating your boundaries clearly.

THE SIGNIFICANCE OF DEFINING BOUNDARIES

What are these mysterious boundaries we keep hearing about? Personal boundaries are like invisible lines that you draw around yourself, defining where you end and where the rest of the world begins. They're a way to protect you and your inner child from harm and ensure that your needs are respected.

Boundaries come in various flavors, just like ice cream! Here are the four main types:

- **Physical boundaries:** Imagine a bubble around you. This is your personal space, and it's crucial to protect it. Personal space varies from person to person, so pay attention to how close or far you feel comfortable with others. It's okay to say, "I need my space right now," when you feel overwhelmed.
- **Emotional boundaries:** This one's all about expressing your feelings and needs. It's like wearing a "feelings vest." You get to decide what emotions you share with others and when. You can kindly say, "I appreciate your concern, but I'd rather not talk about it right now."
- **Mental boundaries:** Your thoughts and beliefs are precious. Protect them like you would a treasure chest! It's perfectly okay to say, "I'd rather not discuss my beliefs on this topic," if a conversation makes you uncomfortable.
- **Time boundaries:** Your time and energy are valuable resources. Just like a bank account, you decide how you spend these resources. You can say, "I'm not available at

that time, but I can do it later," when someone asks for your time.

The important question to ask is, why do we even need boundaries? Let's have a look:

- **Protection:** Boundaries shield your inner child from harm. They prevent others from overstepping your limits and causing emotional or physical harm.
- **Respect:** Setting boundaries sends a message to others that you value and respect yourself. When you respect your needs, others are more likely to follow suit.
- **Self-care:** Boundaries are an act of self-love. They give you the space and freedom to take care of your inner child's needs, ensuring you don't burn out or become emotionally drained.
- **Healthy relationships:** Boundaries are the glue that holds healthy relationships together. They create a balanced dynamic where both parties feel heard and understood.
- **Clarity and communication:** Boundaries provide clarity in your interactions with others. They help you communicate your needs and expectations, reducing misunderstandings and conflicts.
- **Personal growth:** Healthy boundaries encourage personal growth and self-discovery. They enable you to step out of your comfort zone without compromising your well-being.

- **Resilience:** Boundaries build emotional resilience, helping you bounce back from setbacks and challenges. They provide a buffer against negativity and toxicity.
- **Balanced priorities:** Boundaries help you balance your commitments and responsibilities. They ensure that you don't overextend yourself and have time for self-care and the things you love.

THE DIFFERENCE BETWEEN HEALTHY AND UNHEALTHY BOUNDARIES

It's important that we understand the difference between healthy and unhealthy boundaries. Let's have a closer look:

Healthy boundaries:

- **Clear communication:** Healthy boundaries involve open, honest, and respectful communication. You express your needs, desires, and limits kindly but firmly.
- **Self-care:** They prioritize your well-being and self-care. You know when to say "no" when something doesn't align with your values or drains your energy.
- **Respect for others:** They also respect the boundaries of others. You acknowledge and honor their limits, just as you expect them to honor yours.
- **Flexibility:** Healthy boundaries can adapt to different situations. They're not rigid; instead, they're like a sail that adjusts to the winds of life.

Unhealthy boundaries:

- **Overstepping:** Unhealthy boundaries often involve allowing others to overstep your limits or doing the same to them. This can lead to resentment and discomfort.
- **People-pleasing:** You might have a habit of saying "yes" to everything to avoid conflict or gain approval, even if it's against your best interests.
- **Isolation:** On the flip side, some people build walls so high that they isolate themselves. This can lead to loneliness and missed opportunities for growth and connection.
- **Rigidity:** Unhealthy boundaries can be rigid and inflexible. You might stick to the same patterns, even if they no longer serve you.

Protecting your inner child means recognizing that setting healthy boundaries isn't selfish; it's an act of self-love and self-preservation.

HOW DOES OUR CHILDHOOD IMPACT BOUNDARY DEVELOPMENT?

Think of your younger self as a little sapling. If you were nurtured with love, care, and respect, you likely grew into a sturdy tree with strong, healthy boundaries. But if your childhood environment was turbulent or neglectful, those boundaries might be more like a flimsy picket fence in need of repair.

Our past molds our present, and recognizing this connection is the first step. It's not about blaming anyone; it's about understanding how your experiences have influenced your boundary development. Take a moment to reflect on your early years—the family dynamics, relationships, and any significant events. What patterns do you see? Did you feel safe expressing your needs and opinions? Did anyone respect your personal space and emotions?

Let's try to pinpoint the areas where our boundary garden might be lacking some vibrant blooms. We all have unique blind spots, so don't fret if you find a few. It's all part of healing your inner child.

- **People-pleasing potholes:** Are you a chronic people-pleaser, always putting others' needs before your own? It's a common sign of weak boundaries. Remember, it's okay to say no and prioritize your well-being.
- **Emotional overload:** Do you often find yourself overwhelmed by the emotions of others, absorbing their stress like a sponge? This could be a sign that your emotional boundaries need some extra love.
- **Invasion of personal space:** If you feel like people are constantly invading your personal space, physically or emotionally, it's a clue that you might need to reinforce those boundaries.
- **Tolerating disrespect:** Are you tolerating disrespectful or hurtful behavior from others without speaking up? Your inner child deserves respect, and so do you.

Let's have a look back at those formative years. What experiences might have contributed to your boundary issues? Did you grow up in an environment where your feelings were dismissed? Were there moments when your personal space was violated? Did you witness unhealthy relationships around you? These experiences can be like little weeds that sprouted in your boundary garden.

Remember, we're not dwelling on the past to blame or hold grudges. We're shining a light on those weeds so we can start pulling them out and make room for beautiful, healthy boundaries to flourish.

Understanding why boundaries are essential for your inner child is like laying the foundation for a sturdy house. Recognizing the impact of your childhood experiences on your boundary development, identifying those areas where boundaries need reinforcement, and reflecting on the past experiences that shaped you are all vital steps in this healing journey.

RECOGNIZING SIGNS OF BOUNDARY EROSION OR VIOLATION AND MAINTAINING THEM

Can you recognize signs of boundary erosion? In life, boundary erosion can take many forms. It might be someone who constantly invades your privacy, disrespects your opinions, or manipulates your emotions. These situations can be draining, but recognizing them is the first step to healing. So, keep an eye out for those uncomfortable feelings—they're your inner child's way of saying, "Hey, something's not right here."

Setting boundaries might seem intimidating, but it's all about advocating for yourself in a respectful way. Start by acknowledging your feelings and needs. Your inner child's needs are just as valid as anyone else's.

When it's time to set a boundary, be direct but gentle. You can say something like, "I really need some alone time right now," or "I don't appreciate it when you speak to me that way." Remember, it's okay to stand up for yourself, and you don't owe anyone an apology for protecting your inner child.

So, how do we maintain our boundaries over time? It's not a one-and-done thing; it's an ongoing practice. Start by being consistent. If you let a boundary slide once, it becomes easier for others to disregard it in the future.

Surround yourself with people who respect your boundaries. Your inner child deserves to be in the company of those who uplift and support you, not those who constantly push your limits. If someone repeatedly disrespects your boundaries, consider whether that relationship is worth your emotional well-being.

Lastly, be patient with yourself. Setting and maintaining boundaries can be a learning curve. You might stumble along the way, and that's perfectly okay. It's all part of the ride to healing your inner child.

STEP SIX—THE BOUNDARY LINE | 175

DESIGNING A PERSONALIZED PROTECTION PLAN FOR YOUR INNER CHILD

You need to design a protection plan tailor-made for your inner child. Take some time to reflect on what makes you feel safe and respected. What behaviors from others trigger discomfort? What do you need to feel secure? Maybe it's clear communication, space when you need it, or simply saying no when you want to. Once you've got your blueprint, it's time to put it into action.

Remember, your inner child deserves this protection, and it's perfectly okay to prioritize your well-being.

Your inner child's safety comes first. Be clear and assertive about your boundaries, and don't be swayed by guilt or manipulation. Healthy relationships respect your boundaries. If someone resists, it might be a sign that they're not a good fit for your inner circle.

Sometimes, the biggest challenge in setting boundaries is dealing with your inner resistance. You might second-guess yourself, worry about hurting others' feelings, or feel guilty. That's okay; it's perfectly normal.

To address this inner resistance, remind yourself that boundaries are a form of self-love. You're taking care of yourself, just like a loving parent would. Be kind to yourself, and remember that you deserve respect and protection.

When you start enforcing your boundaries, you might feel uncomfortable or vulnerable. That's okay, too. Growth often happens outside your comfort zone. Embrace that discomfort as a sign that you're doing something brave and transformative.

Lean on your support system, whether it's friends, family, or a therapist. They can help you navigate those choppy waters and offer a lifeline when things get tough.

Design your protection plan, stand your ground in the face of pushback, address your inner resistance, and remember that managing discomfort is a part of the healing process.

INTERACTIVE ELEMENT

How often have you felt like your boundaries were being crossed? Have you really given this much thought? We know when it happens; we don't like it, but do we know how often, when, or why?

For this exercise, I would like you to take a moment and grab a notebook or open a notes app on your phone. I want you to jot down actual situations where you've felt your boundaries were crossed.

- That friend who constantly drains your energy.
- A family member who expects you to always say yes.
- A colleague who doesn't respect your input.
- A partner who pushes your limits.

Done? Great! Now, read through that list again and ask yourself this important question. What would happen if I enforced my boundaries around this situation? You would be giving yourself the best gift.

I want you to take your list of crossed boundaries and use it as a starting point. Start setting those boundaries: Protect your inner child and watch how your life transforms. Remember, it's not about building walls; it's about creating a safe and nurturing space where your inner child can flourish.

Journal Prompts

1. Consider a healthy boundary you'd like to establish from your list. What specific actions can you take to communicate and enforce this boundary in a respectful and assertive manner?
2. What do you think contributes to you allowing your boundaries to be crossed repeatedly?
3. What is holding you back from enforcing and communicating your boundaries? Fear, guilt, or discomfort?
4. What are some positive experiences where setting boundaries enhanced your well-being? What lessons can you draw from these instances when setting boundaries in the future?

As we wrap up Step 6 in this chapter, I want you to carry with you the knowledge that boundaries are a gift you give to your inner child, a promise to protect and nurture them.

In the next chapter with Step 7, we'll explore the art of letting go of the past. Together, we'll learn how to release the burdens of yesterday, making room for a brighter, more joyful future.

11

STEP SEVEN—LETTING GO OF THE PAST

Forgiveness is giving up the hope that the past could have been any different, but we cannot move forward if we're still holding onto the pain of that past and wishing it was something else.

— OPRAH WINFREY

It is time to explore the incredible power of forgiveness and the art of releasing the burdens weighing you down. In this chapter, I'll show you how to untangle those knots of pain so you can finally stop reliving those old wounds and break free from the grip of the past. Until you release that pain, it has a sneaky way of showing up and causing more hurt in your present.

Our inner child is that part of us that holds onto all the hurt, pain, and trauma we've experienced in our past. It's like a little version of ourselves still carrying the baggage from years ago. And when we don't let go or forgive, that baggage can weigh us down in ways we may not even realize.

Now, imagine a woman named Kris. She's a mom of three beautiful children, but she's struggling because she grew up with a toxic mother. Her mother's constant criticism and emotional abuse left deep scars on Kris's inner child. As she became a mother herself, she noticed that she was repeating the same hurtful patterns with her kids. She was caught in a cycle of negativity that she desperately wanted to break.

Kris realized that to be the loving and nurturing mother she wanted to be and to give her children the life they deserved, she had to confront her past. She had to forgive her toxic mother, not for her mom's sake, but for her inner peace and the future of her children.

Letting go of resentment and bitterness can feel like shedding a heavy coat you've been wearing for years. It's not easy, but it's necessary for your emotional freedom. Kris started by reflecting on her childhood, acknowledging the pain she felt, and allowing herself to grieve for the childhood she never had.

Visualize this with me: Kris sat down in a quiet room, closed her eyes, and pictured herself as a child, hurt and confused. She saw her toxic mother in front of her and imagined saying the words, "I forgive you." It wasn't about condoning her mother's actions; it was about releasing the grip that pain had on her heart.

As Kris forgave, she felt a weight lift off her shoulders. It was like a ray of sunshine breaking through the clouds. She could breathe easier, and she started to feel a sense of inner peace she hadn't experienced in years.

And here's the beautiful part of this story: as Kris healed her inner child and forgave her past, she broke the generational cycle of toxicity. She learned to parent her children with love and kindness, giving them the life she had always wished for herself. Her journey wasn't always smooth, but the transformation was remarkable.

I believe in you, and I know that you, like Kris, can find the strength to let go and forgive. It's a powerful step toward the life you truly deserve, one filled with love, happiness, and inner peace.

WHAT IS FORGIVENESS AND HOW DO WE FORGIVE?

Forgiveness is like a magic wand that can transform your life. It's not about condoning hurtful actions or letting anyone off the hook. Instead, it's about releasing the heavy burden of anger, resentment, and pain you've been carrying around. Forgiveness is setting yourself free from the emotional shackles that hold you back.

A great question to ponder is, why would we need to forgive ourselves? We all make mistakes; there is no escaping that. But sometimes, we cling to those mistakes, beating ourselves up over them for years. This self-blame can keep you stuck in the past, preventing you from embracing the present and future.

Forgiving yourself is an act of self-compassion. It's about acknowledging your mistakes, learning from them, and choosing to move forward with love and understanding. When you forgive yourself, you make space for healing and growth. Remember, you deserve forgiveness as much as anyone else.

Then the next question should be, but how do we forgive ourselves? Forgiving yourself isn't always easy, but it's entirely possible. Here are some steps to help you along the way:

- **Acknowledge your feelings:** Start by recognizing the emotions you're holding onto. What are you blaming yourself for? Allow yourself to feel these emotions without judgment.
- **Self-reflection:** Reflect on why you made those choices or mistakes in the past. What was going on in your life at that time? Understanding the context can help you let go.
- **Learn and grow:** Use your past as a teacher. What lessons have you learned from your mistakes? How have you grown and evolved as a person? This perspective can be empowering.
- **Self-compassion:** Have you ever had a conversation with a great friend who is struggling with a bad choice they made? I have no doubt you were supportive and compassionate, reminding them they needed to forgive themselves. That is exactly the compassion you need to show yourself now.

Forgiveness can be tough, especially when the wounds run deep. If you're struggling to forgive, that's okay. Here's what you can do:

- **Create a forgiveness ritual:** Light a candle, burn some incense, or find a peaceful spot in nature. Perform a ritual or ceremony where you symbolically release the negative emotions tied to the person or situation you're forgiving. Imagine the burdens lifting away as you do this.

- **Visualize forgiveness:** Close your eyes and visualize a scene where you and the person you need to forgive are at peace. Picture yourselves lighter, forgiving, and letting go of any negative feelings. Visualization can help reprogram your mind toward forgiveness.

- **Artistic expression:** Use art to process and express your feelings. Paint, draw, sculpt, or create any form of art representing your journey toward forgiveness. Sometimes, the act of creating can be incredibly therapeutic.

- **Empathy exercise:** Put yourself in the shoes of the person you're forgiving, even if that's you. Try to understand their perspective and what might have led them to their actions. This can help you develop empathy, which is a key component of forgiveness.

- **Meditation and mindfulness:** Practice forgiveness meditation, where you focus on letting go of resentment and replacing it with compassion. Mindfulness can help you become aware of your feelings without judgment, making it easier to forgive.

- **Symbolic gesture:** Create a symbolic gesture to represent forgiveness. It could be planting a tree or even donating to a charity in the name of the person you're forgiving. Remember, this can also be you! This physical act can be a powerful symbol of your forgiveness.

HOW TO LET GO OF SHAME AND GUILT

Let's start by understanding what shame and guilt really are.

Shame is that heavy feeling that you're inherently flawed or unworthy. It often stems from past experiences, especially during childhood, when you may have been made to feel inadequate or less than others. Shame can make you believe that you are fundamentally a bad person, and it can be a deeply painful emotion to carry.

Guilt, on the other hand, is more about feeling remorse for a specific action or behavior. It's a signal that you've done something that doesn't align with your values or has hurt someone. Guilt can actually be a healthy emotion when it prompts you to make amends or change your behavior. However, it can become something destructive when it becomes excessive or chronic.

Now, here's how you can begin to move on from shame and guilt:

- **Acknowledge your feelings:** The first step is to recognize and accept that you are feeling shame or guilt. Sometimes, we try to bury these emotions, but acknowledging them is essential to start the healing process.

- **Identify the source:** Try to pinpoint the source of your shame or guilt. Was it something from your past or a recent event? Understanding where these feelings are coming from can help you address them more effectively.
- **Learn and grow:** If your guilt is related to a specific action, use it as an opportunity for personal growth. Apologize if necessary and take steps to prevent similar mistakes in the future. This can be incredibly empowering.
- **Challenge negative beliefs:** Challenge those negative beliefs about yourself that shame has ingrained in your mind. Remind yourself of your strengths, accomplishments, and the times you've done good things.
- **Practice self-forgiveness:** Forgiving yourself is a powerful act of self-love. Understand that nothing you did in your past has to determine who you are today or in the future. You have the capacity to change and grow.
- **Mindfulness and meditation:** These practices can help you stay grounded in the present moment and reduce the grip of shame and guilt from the past. They can also help you develop a more compassionate attitude toward yourself.

Remember, healing your inner child and letting go of shame and guilt is a process, and it may not happen overnight. But with patience, self-compassion, and the willingness to confront

186 | REPARENTING YOUR WOUNDED INNER CHILD

these emotions head-on, you can find your way to a place of healing and self-acceptance.

INTERACTIVE ELEMENT

I would like to take you through a practical three-step forgiveness exercise that you can apply to various situations in your life.

Step One: The Conversation Step—Speak and Listen

Begin by telling your younger self that you understand their pain and that you're there to support them. Share a memory or situation you'd like to address. It is best to be as specific as possible.

For example, "Remember when dad ruined our birthday party because he was drunk, violent, and threw our cake? I know it hurt."

Now, listen to your inner child. They might express their sadness, anger, or resentment. It's essential to validate their feelings. Respond with kindness and empathy, like, "It's okay to feel that way. I'm here with you now, and I love you."

Step Two: Plant a Seed of Forgiveness

What you'll need: A small seed, like a sunflower or basil seed, and a pot of soil.

How to do it:

- Holding the seed in your hand, think about the person or situation you're forgiving.
- As you plant the seed into the soil, imagine burying the negative feelings and emotions.
- As the plant grows, it'll be a living testament to your act of forgiveness and healing. If you are forgiving yourself, you should envision the growth you are experiencing from self-forgiveness. Each time you water and nurture it, you're nurturing your inner growth too.

Step Three: The Release Ritual

This step is about symbolically releasing the past. Once you've conversed and connected with your inner child, write a letter to them, reminding them you know their hurt and pain. Depending on what feels right for you:

- Burn it, watching as the flames consume the words, imagining them transforming into healing energy.
- Or, bury it deep in the earth, allowing Mother Nature to cradle and transform that energy.

When you're done, take a moment. Breathe deeply. Feel the lightness that comes from understanding and letting go.

Journal Prompts

1. Define what forgiveness means to you. How can forgiving yourself and others contribute to your inner child's healing journey?
2. Consider the impact of holding onto past grievances. How does it affect your present relationships and overall happiness?
3. Explore forgiveness as a form of self-liberation. How does forgiving others free you from the emotional burden of the past?
4. What guilt and shame have you carried with you from childhood? What steps can you take to release their hold on you?
5. Consider the role of self-forgiveness in your healing journey. What aspects of yourself do you find challenging to forgive, and how can you work towards self-acceptance?

In this pivotal chapter on letting go, Step 7 had us looking into the recesses of our hearts, learning how to forgive ourselves and those around us for the past wounds and fears that have held us back. As we stand at the threshold of the final chapters, poised to embrace continual growth, let us carry with us the wisdom gained from releasing the burdens of our past.

PART III

FACING FORWARD

12

GROWING FROM STRENGTH TO STRENGTH

Vulnerability is not winning or losing; it's having the courage to show up and be seen when we have no control over the outcome. Vulnerability is not weakness; it's our greatest measure of courage.

— BRENEE BROWN

We're talking about something truly empowering: embracing our strength. By embracing continual growth, vulnerability, and resiliency, we're not just growing older; we're growing wiser, kinder, and stronger. You see, we live in a world where we've been told that strong people are like rock faces: silent, hard, and unyielding. But guess what? We're about to shatter that myth. True strength, the kind that resides deep within each of us lies in being flexible, yielding, and open to learning.

HOW EMBRACING AND NURTURING OUR INNER CHILD HELPS

Your inner child holds the key to many aspects of your adult life, and by taking care of that young, vulnerable part of yourself, you can experience profound transformation.

Think of it like this: your inner child carries memories, emotions, and experiences from your past that may still influence your present. By acknowledging and healing those wounds, you create space for growth, self-compassion, and genuine connections with both yourself and others. It's as if you're giving your inner child a warm, reassuring place to heal.

Here's why embracing and nurturing this inner child is such a powerful and healing experience:

- **Self-discovery:** Our inner child carries the essence of who we truly are before life's challenges and societal expectations shaped us. By reconnecting with this part of ourselves, we can uncover our authentic desires, passions, and values. It's like rediscovering a hidden treasure within.
- **Emotional healing:** Many of us carry unresolved emotions from childhood—pain, sadness, anger, or even joy that was never fully expressed. Embracing our inner child allows us to release these emotions in a

healthy way, promoting emotional healing and mental well-being.

- **Improved relationships:** As we nurture and heal our inner child, we become better at understanding our emotional needs. This newfound awareness can greatly enhance our relationships. We learn to communicate our feelings more effectively and build deeper connections with others.

- **Resilience:** Your inner child holds the seeds of your resilience. By nurturing this part of yourself, you tap into a wellspring of strength that can help you cope with life's challenges more gracefully. It's like having an inner cheerleader who believes in your ability to overcome anything.

- **Healing the past**: Many of us carry wounds from childhood—experiences that left scars on our hearts. Embracing and nurturing our inner child allows us to revisit these painful memories, not to relive the pain but to heal it. It's like offering a soothing embrace to the child within, telling them it's okay and they are loved.

EMBRACE VULNERABILITY

You know, when it comes to healing our inner child, embracing vulnerability can make all the difference. But first, let's clear up what vulnerability is and what it isn't. Vulnerability isn't weakness. It's not about being a pushover or exposing yourself to harm. It's about courageously showing your true self with all your imperfections, fears, and feelings. Vulnerability is like opening the door to your inner world, letting the light in.

Now, let's talk about the power of being vulnerable in the healing process. When you allow yourself to be vulnerable, you create space for growth and connection. It's like tending to a wound—exposing it to fresh air and sunlight helps it heal. Similarly, sharing your vulnerabilities allows you to heal emotional wounds and build deeper connections with yourself and others.

But why is vulnerability so important? Well, it's the gateway to authenticity and self-acceptance. When you embrace vulnerability, you acknowledge your humanity. You give yourself permission to feel and be imperfect, and that's where the magic happens. You start to understand your inner child's needs, fears, and desires, which is crucial for healing and self-growth.

Now, let's talk about how to be safely vulnerable. Safety is key here, and it begins with choosing the right people to open up to. Seek out those who've proven themselves trustworthy and understanding. Start small, sharing your feelings gradually, testing the waters. Remember, it's okay to set boundaries and say no if you're not ready.

EMBRACE RESILIENCY

So, what exactly is resiliency? Think of it as your inner power, your ability to bounce back when life gets messy. It's that unwavering strength that helps you not just survive but thrive in challenging times.

Let's ask ourselves, how do we overcome adversity? Resiliency is your shield, your secret weapon against life's ups and downs.

When you embrace it, you're better equipped to weather the storms that come your way.

But how do you become more resilient? It starts with letting go of that victim mentality. Here are five steps to help you cultivate a more resilient mindset and life:

- **Self-awareness:** Understand your strengths and weaknesses. Knowing yourself is the first step toward building resilience.
- **Acceptance:** Embrace your past and acknowledge that it has shaped who you are today. Acceptance is the foundation of growth.
- **Adaptability:** Life is full of surprises. Learn to adapt to change and see it as an opportunity for growth, not a threat.
- **Problem-solving:** Instead of dwelling on problems, focus on finding solutions. A proactive approach is key to resilience.
- **Learn from setbacks:** Failure is not the end; it's a lesson. Analyze what went wrong and use it as a stepping stone for future success.

By following these steps, you can shed that victim mentality and step into your personal power. You'll discover a well of strength within you that you never knew existed. Remember, you are stronger than you think, and resilience is your superpower.

INTERACTIVE ELEMENT

I would like you to try a resilience self-assessment. It's a simple yet powerful tool that can shed light on your strengths and areas for improvement. Remember, there's no judgment here— just a chance to learn more about yourself.

So, on a scale from 1 to 4, with 1 meaning "Never or Rarely" and 4 meaning "Always." Let's go through these 13 questions:

1. Do you have someone you trust and can turn to for support? Rate yourself.
2. How often do you contribute to the well-being of others?
3. Are you taking good care of your body, from exercise to sleep and a balanced diet?
4. Do you regularly engage in practices that calm your mind and body?
5. When facing challenges, do you consider multiple perspectives and options?
6. How much trust do you have in yourself, your intuition, and your abilities?
7. Are you open to new and unfamiliar experiences?
8. Do you approach challenges believing you can work through them?
9. Are you mindful of the world around you, and can you anticipate opportunities and challenges?
10. Have you tackled difficult challenges before and found healthy ways to overcome them?

11. When challenges arise, do you face them head-on without denial or avoidance?

12. Are you involved in activities that deeply satisfy you and focus your attention?

13. Can you maintain perspective on your challenges by considering the bigger picture?

How to Interpret the Scores

- **If you score 36 or higher:** You believe yourself to be resilient. It's probable that you'll not only thrive when confronted with challenges but also have the potential to become a robust source of support and an inspiring role model for those around you.

- **If you score 27–35:** You believe you are on resilience most of the time, suggesting that you're likely to handle most challenges adequately. There's potential for you to strengthen your resilience.

- **If you score 26 or lower:** You don't believe you are resilient at all. You have a lot of room for improvement. This score is normal in those who haven't faced challenges in childhood or have been inundated with them.

As you go through these questions, be gentle with yourself. There's no rush and no need to be perfect.

As we conclude this chapter on embracing resiliency and growth, it's important to recognize that we've explored the incredible strength that resides within us, and we've identified areas where we can continue to nurture and expand that strength.

13

CELEBRATING AND POWERFULLY CREATING

The most beautiful things are not associated with money; they are memories and moments. If you don't celebrate those, they can pass you by.

— ALEK WEK

It is time to learn how to foster a mindset that not only celebrates our successes but also welcomes our failures as valuable stepping stones on our path to personal growth. It's all about learning to dance with joy and power, and with every thought, word, action, reflection, or aha moment, you'll find yourself becoming a more resilient, joyful, and empowered person.

WHY DO WE NEED TO CELEBRATE?

Celebration is like a warm hug for your soul. It's a joyful acknowledgment of your progress and achievements along the way.

So, how does celebration help us on our healing journey?

- **Boosts confidence:** Celebrating your achievements, big or small, boosts your self-confidence. It reminds you that you're capable and you've come a long way.
- **Motivates progress:** When you celebrate your personal growth, it fuels your motivation to keep going. You start to see the positive impact of your efforts, which encourages you to continue the journey.
- **Fosters self-compassion:** Celebrating your progress is an act of self-compassion. It sends the message that you value yourself and your healing journey. It's a way of saying, "I matter, and my growth matters."

Now, let's talk about some unique ways to celebrate your personal growth:

- **Create a vision board:** Craft a vision board filled with images and quotes representing your dreams and aspirations. When you achieve a milestone on your healing journey, add a symbol or a note to your board. Seeing it grow over time can be incredibly motivating and celebratory.

- **Dance it out:** Put on your favorite music and have a solo dance party. Dancing is a fantastic way to release pent-up emotions and celebrate your vitality. Let loose and enjoy the moment.
- **Plant a symbolic garden:** Plant a real or symbolic garden to represent your growth. Each time you make progress, add a flower, stone, or decorative item to your garden. Watching it flourish is a beautiful reminder of your inner strength.
- **Host a "me-day":** Dedicate an entire day to yourself. Do activities that bring you joy, whether going for a hike, visiting a museum, or simply indulging in your favorite book. This day is all about celebrating you and your journey.

EMBRACING TRANSFORMATIVE GROWTH AND WHOLENESS

Let's focus on maintaining a growth mindset. This is the foundation for healing our inner child. A growth mindset is all about believing in our ability to change and grow, no matter what life throws at us.

One key aspect of a growth mindset is embracing challenges. Instead of seeing them as roadblocks, see them as opportunities for growth. Another important element is self-compassion. We have touched on this a few times throughout this book because it is important. We need to be mindful of how we speak to ourselves. Acknowledge that perfection is a myth. Self-compassion allows you to forgive yourself for past mistakes and move forward with love and understanding.

So, how do we stay motivated for the long haul?

We talked about the importance of celebrating your progress at every level. This keeps your motivation alive and reminds you that you're making continuous strides toward healing your inner child.

Throughout these pages, we talked about building that supportive community. Share your journey with friends or a therapist who can provide encouragement and guidance. Knowing that you're not alone can be incredibly motivating and comforting.

Additionally, stay curious and open-minded. Embrace the idea that there's always more to learn about yourself and the world around you. This curiosity will keep you engaged and excited about your personal growth.

And lastly, remember to take breaks and practice self-care. These chapters are filled with reminders about the importance of recharging your emotional batteries. Whether through meditation, hobbies, or simply walking in nature, self-care helps you stay balanced and motivated.

KEEP THE INNER CHILD HEALING GOING

You've already taken a significant step in acknowledging the existence of your inner child, and that's fantastic. Throughout this book, we have spent significant time and effort revealing why healing and moving forward is crucial. Now, let's make it an effortless part of your everyday life.

- **Create daily rituals:** The best way to make inner child work a natural part of your life is to turn it into a daily ritual. Just like brushing your teeth or having your morning coffee, set aside a few minutes each day to connect with your inner child. This can be through meditation, journaling, or even simply reflecting on your feelings.
- **Keep up your journal:** Use your journaling as a fantastic tool to track your progress and emotions. Keep writing down your experiences with your inner child, your goals, and any revelations you have along the way. This will help you stay committed to your inner child's growth.
- **Adjust as needed:** Life is dynamic, and so is your inner child's work. Be flexible and adjust your approach when necessary. Don't be too hard on yourself if you miss a day or encounter setbacks. Healing is a lifelong process.
- **Embrace your authentic self:** The more you connect with your inner child, the closer you come to your authentic self. Embrace this beautiful journey of self-discovery, and remember that you are growing stronger with each step.

INTERACTIVE ELEMENT

You are stronger than you realize. List your newfound strengths:

- Make a list of the strengths you've discovered within yourself throughout this healing journey. It could be your resilience, compassion, determination, or any other qualities that have surfaced.

Why not start a Success Journal?

- Each evening, take a few minutes to jot down three things you got right that day. It could be as simple as making your bed, showing kindness to someone, or taking care of yourself.

Journal Prompts

1. Think about and write down the changes you've made in your life. Maybe you've set boundaries with people who were toxic, or perhaps you've started a new hobby that brings you joy.
2. How do these changes make you feel? Write down your thoughts and emotions. Embrace the positive feelings that come with these changes.
3. Acknowledge and write down any challenges you've faced. This process can help you recognize your growth and appreciate the strength it took to make those changes.

4. What aspects of your life would you like to improve further?

5. What dreams and aspirations are waiting to be pursued?

This practice helps you focus on your achievements and reinforces your sense of accomplishment. You'll see how your inner strength plays a significant role in these successes.

Remember, your inner child is a part of this process, too. Nurture and support them as you embark on this new chapter in your life. Setting clear goals will give you a sense of purpose and direction, and achieving them will strengthen your belief in yourself.

I want you to carry the wisdom that healing your inner child and cultivating a growth mindset are intertwined journeys. Embracing your past, nurturing your inner child, and fostering a mindset of continuous growth and learning are all part of the beautiful tapestry of your life.

NO ONE WALKS THIS PATH ALONE

Not one of us walks this path alone – and you have a unique opportunity to help someone else realize that.

Simply by sharing your honest opinion of this book and a little about how it has helped you, you'll show new readers where they can find the guidance they need to begin their own healing journey.

WANT TO HELP OTHERS?

Your review can be a beacon of hope for someone who, like you, is seeking a path to self-discovery and personal growth.

Thank you so much for your support. We all need a guiding light sometimes, and your words will make a huge difference.

 **Scan the QR code to leave your review!**

CONCLUSION

As you reach the conclusion of this transformative voyage through these pages, I want to express my heartfelt gratitude and admiration for your commitment to healing, growth, and self-discovery. You've shown incredible courage by embarking on this path, and I hope you're already beginning to feel the positive changes in your life.

Throughout this book, we've explored the profound world of childhood and generational trauma, uncovering the roots of destructive patterns that may have held you back for far too long. Together, we've walked through seven empowering steps that have equipped you with the tools and insights necessary to not only break free from those patterns but also to build emotional strength and experience personal growth.

Each step you've taken, every revelation you've had, is a testament to your strength and resilience. The fact that you've reached this conclusion is a monumental achievement. You've shown up for yourself, and that's something to be immensely proud of.

In moments of doubt or when facing challenges on your ongoing journey, I encourage you to revisit the sections of this book that resonate most with you. The wisdom and guidance you've discovered here are always at your fingertips, ready to offer support and guidance whenever needed.

Never forget that you are worthy of love, healing, and happiness. You deserve a life free from the burdens of your past. You are seen, heard, and loved—by yourself and by those who have walked this path with you.

As you move forward from this point, may you nurture and reparent your wounded inner child, embracing the beautiful journey of self-discovery and transformation ahead. Remember, you have all the tools you need within you, and you are never alone on this path.

Other Books You'll Love By

Leigh W. Hart

Available Now

Available April 2024

Elevate Your Journey With...

EXCLUSIVE COMPLIMENTARY
SUPPORT MATERIALS!

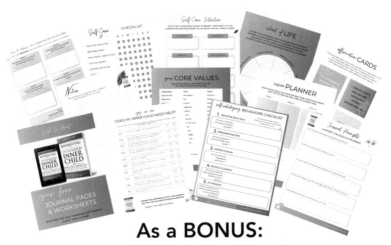

As a BONUS:

I have created a customized collection of
75+ journal pages and interactive worksheets that have been
designed to complement the steps, journal prompts, and exercises
discussed in this book perfectly.

Go to:
InnerChild.LeighWHart.com
to receive your FREE
printable support materials.

REFERENCES

Amos, T. (n.d.) *Tori Amos quotes*. Brainy Quote. https://www.brainyquote. com/quotes/tori_amos_183441

Attachment trauma: How childhood trauma can shape your attachment style as told by a therapist. (2022, August 25). White Rock Therapy. https://www.white rocktherapy.net/blog/attachment-trauma-how-childhood-trauma-can-shape-your-attachment-style-as-told-by-a-therapist

Best 15 inner child healing exercises to reparent your inner child (+ FREE inner child worksheets PDF). (2023, September 25). Ineffable LIving. https://ineffable living.com/inner-child-exercises/#29-inner-child-healing-exercises-pdf

Bardugo, L. (n.d.) *Leigh Bardugo quotes*. Goodreads. https://www.goodreads. com/quotes/8119864-stop-treating-your-pain-like-it-s-something-you-imagined-if

Brown, B. (n.d.). *Brene Brown quotes*. Happier Human. https://www.happierhu man.com/brene-brown-quotes/#:

Carter-Sobell, L. (n.d.). *Exercise on identifying triggers.* https://www.nova.edu/ gsc/forms/client_handout_4_6_exercise_on_identifying_triggers.pdf

Chan, Y. K.. (n.d.). *Yong Kang Chan quotes*. Goodreads. https://www.goodreads. com/work/quotes/63896837-parent-yourself-again-love-yourself-the-way-you-have-always-wanted-to-be

Chen, L. (2015, October 19). *7 things your inner child needs to hear you say.* Tiny Buddha. https://tinybuddha.com/blog/7-things-your-inner-child-needs-to-hear-you-say/

Child maltreatment. (2022, September 19). World Health Organization. https:// www.who.int/news-room/fact-sheets/detail/child-maltreatment

Chopra, D. (n.d.). *Deepak Chopra's 7-step exercise to release emotional turbulence.* Gaiam. https://www.gaiam.com/blogs/discover/deepak-chopras-7-step-exercise-to-release-emotional-turbulence

Cikanavičius, D. (2018, September 2). *A brief guide to unprocessed childhood toxic shame.* Psych Central. https://psychcentral.com/blog/psychology-self/ 2018/09/childhood-toxic-shame#1

Cooks-Campbell, A. (2022, March 15). *How inner child work enables healing and playful discovery.* BetterUp. https://www.betterup.com/blog/inner-child-work#:

Coron, J. (n.d.). *Jeanette Coron quotes.* PsychCentral. https://psychcentral.com/health/quotes-healthy-boundaries#the-need-for-boundaries

Costillo, L. (2023, October 15). *Emotional intelligence statistics.* Gitex. https://blog.gitnux.com/emotional-intelligence-statistics/

Crouch, S. (2011, June 2). *How to let go of the need for approval to start thriving.* Tiny Buddha. https://tinybuddha.com/blog/how-to-let-go-of-the-need-for-approval-to-start-thriving/

Davenport, B. (2023, March 5). *Mindfully heal your inner child with these 11 essential exercises + worksheets.* Mindful Zen. https://mindfulzen.co/inner-child-healing-exercises/

Davis, A. (2023, September 18). 80 Healing Inner Child Quotes to Feel Validated. Ambitiously Alexa. https://ambitiouslyalexa.com/healing-inner-child-quotes/

Diukman, Y. (2022, May 12). *19 eye-opening rumi quotes for navigating the maze of life.* BookRetreats. https://bookretreats.com/blog/19-eye-opening-rumi-quotes-for-navigating-the-maze-of-life/

Factsheet 10: How our thoughts govern how we feel. (n.d.). MyGriefAssist. https://www.mygriefassist.com.au/factsheets/factsheet-10-how-our-thoughts-govern-how-we-feel/

Forgeard, V. (2022, October 1). *59 inner child journal prompts to help you unleash your creativity and have fun!* https://brilliantio.com/inner-child-journal-prompts/

4 ways to boost your self-compassion. (2021, February 12). Harvard Health Publishing. https://www.health.harvard.edu/mental-health/4-ways-to-boost-your-self-compassion

Goleman, D. (n.d.). *Daniel Goleman quotes.* Center for Building a Culture of Empathy. http://cultureofempathy.com/References/Experts/Daniel-Goleman.htm

Gregory, A. (2020, November 18). *Re-parenting my inner child: My journey of healing from childhood neglect.* OC87 Recovery Diaries. https://oc87recoverydiaries.org/childhood-neglect/

GoodTherapy. (2022, January 24). *Why should I go to therapy? 8 signs it's time to see a therapist.* GoodTherapy.org Therapy Blog. https://www.goodtherapy.org/blog/why-should-i-go-to-therapy-8-signs-its-time-to-see-a-therapist

Gowmon, V. (n.d.). *Vince Gowmon quotes.* Kidadl. https://kidadl.com/quotes/

top-inner-child-quotes-to-help-you-hea

Haupt, A. (2023, April 6). *What to know about inner child work.* Time. https://time.com/6268636/inner-child-work-healing/

Johnson, E. B. (2022, July 19). *These key misconceptions about childhood trauma prevent you from healing.* Practical Growth. https://medium.com/practical-growth/these-key-misconceptions-about-childhood-trauma-prevent-you-from-healing-56c6b7eefb9d

Joynson, S. H. (2022, May 16). *How to stop neglecting and abusing your inner child.* Tiny Buddha. https://tinybuddha.com/blog/stop-abusing-inner-child-practice-self-love-instead/

Jung, C. (n.d.). *Carl Jung quotes.* A-Z Quotes. https://www.azquotes.com/author/7659-Carl_Jung/tag/children

Jung, C. G. (n.d.). *Carl Gustav Jung.* Goodreads. https://www.goodreads.com/quotes/11125-whatever-is-rejected-from-the-self-appears-in-the-world

King, V. (n.d.). *Vex King quotes.* Goodreads. https://www.goodreads.com/work/quotes/88480071-healing-is-the-new-high-a-guide-to-overcoming-emotional-turmoil-and-fin

L, A. (2020, December 11). *How I found my purpose in the healing journey.* The Sidebar. https://medium.com/the-sidebar/how-i-found-my-purpose-in-the-healing-journey-3e81c5924491

Lawson, K. (n.d.). *How do thoughts and emotions affect health?* Taking Charge of Your Health & Wellbeing. https://www.takingcharge.csh.umn.edu/how-do-thoughts-and-emotions-affect-health

Levine, P. (2023, March 10). *What is somatic experiencing?* Somatic Experiencing - Continuing Education. https://traumahealing.org/se-101/

Malhorta, M. (n.d.). *Maddy Malhotra quotes.* The Enemy of Average. https://theenemyofaverage.com/positive-self-talk-quotes/

Meditation For Women. (2019, December 17). *Inner child meditation for healing / meditation for women.* Women's Meditation Network. https://womensmeditationnetwork.com/heal-your-inner-child-meditation/

Mind Tools Content Team. (n.d.-a). *Self-sabotage.* MindTools. https://www.mindtools.com/ano939l/self-sabotage

Mind Tools Content Team. (n.d.-b). *The Holmes and Rahe stress scale.* Www.mindtools.com. https://www.mindtools.com/avn893g/the-holmes-and-rahe-stress-scale

Physical health impacts mental wellbeing. (n.d.) American Veterinary Medical Association. https://www.avma.org/resources-tools/wellbeing/physical-health-impacts-mental-wellbeing

Pikorn, I. (2020, July 1). *Noticing, healing and freeing your inner child.* Insight Timer Blog. https://insighttimer.com/blog/inner-child-meaning-noticing-healing-freeing/

Schaffner, A. K. (2020, June 26). *Core beliefs: Worksheets to challenge negative beliefs.* PositivePsychology.com. https://positivepsychology.com/core-beliefs-worksheets/

Scott, E. (2022, March 31). *How to deal with negative emotions and stress.* Verywell Mind. https://www.verywellmind.com/how-should-i-deal-with-negative-emotions-3144603

Simone, F. (2017, December 4). *Negative self-talk: Don't let it overwhelm you.* Psychology Today. https://www.psychologytoday.com/us/blog/family-affair/201712/negative-self-talk-dont-let-it-overwhelm-you

Story and testimonials - Inner child work & healing from within. (2019, June 8). Wellness Space. https://wellness-space.net/story-and-testimonials-inner-child-work-healing-from-within/

Terlizzi, E. P., & Zablotsky, B. (2020, September). *Mental health treatment among adults: United States, 2019.* CDC Centers for Disease Control and Prevention. https://www.cdc.gov/nchs/products/databriefs/db380.htm

Tolle, E. (2023, May 2). Falling below and rising above thought . Eckhart Tolle | Official Site - Spiritual Teachings and Tools for Personal Growth and Happiness. https://eckharttolle.com/falling-below-and-rising-above-thought/

Trauma. (2021, November 11). Mental Health Foundation. https://www.mentalhealth.org.uk/explore-mental-health/a-z-topics/trauma#:

Tucker, S. (2023, September 10). *Reparenting yourself exercises embrace self healing and nurture your inner child.* Generation Mindful. https://genmindful.com/blogs/mindful-moments/reparenting-yourself-exercises

Understanding child trauma. (2023, March 17). SAMHSA. https://www.samhsa.gov/child-trauma/understanding-child-trauma

Weingus, L. (2022, May 17). *45 Journaling prompts to help heal your inner child and unleash joy.* Silk + Sonder. https://www.silkandsonder.com/blogs/news/inner-child-journal-prompts

Wek, A. (n.d.). *Alek Wek quotes.* BrainyQuote. https://www.brainyquote.com/quotes/alek_wek_783092

What is EMDR? (2022, October 20). EMDR Institute, Inc.. https://www.emdr.com/what-is-emdr/

Winfrey, O. (n.d.). Oprah Winfrey quotes. QuoteFancy. https://quotefancy.
com/quote/879440/Oprah-Winfrey-Forgiveness-is-giving-up-the-hope-
that-the-past-could-have-been-any#:

Made in the USA
Thornton, CO
06/03/24 16:09:30

708ecde9-afb4-40f8-a8c1-d0e5e257b82cR01